CBT & MINDFULNESS ANXIETY TOOLKIT FOR BEGINNERS

SELF HELP MANUAL - MINDFULNESS AND MEDITATION FOR ANXIETY : EFT & TAPPING : COGNITIVE BEHAVIORAL THERAPY FOR ANXIETY : 3 GUIDED MEDITATION SCRIPTS

PAUL ROGERS

ROBERT BLOOM

MINDFULNESS AND MEDITATION FOR ANXIETY

DISCOVER THE POWER OF MINDFUL THINKING AND MEDITATION TO REDUCE ANXIOUS THOUGHTS, DECLUTTER YOUR MIND AND RELIEVE STRESS

MINDFULNESS & MEDITATION
FOR ANXIETY

Discover the Power of Mindful Thinking and Meditation
To Reduce Anxious Thoughts,
Declutter Your Mind and Relieve Stress

PAUL ROGERS

INTRODUCTION

We all worry.

It doesn't matter whether we admit it or not, it's still true.

Some of us worry about significant things in our lives, like our relationships, our job or our life's direction. Some of us, on the other hand, worry about less significant things, like what items are on our to-do list or something we said or failed to say.

Worrying is completely normal. We worry when our mind is trying to work out something specific. Worry is the brain's way to solve a problem. Worry can last for minutes or days. We can usually control worry, rather than worry controlling us.

Anxiety, however, is different. We experience anxiety in our bodies, more than in our minds. Our anxiety tends not to be related to a specific problem.

Anxiety is rarely productive. It can last for weeks or months. Anxiety is often out of our control. It's all-pervasive and anxiety can be very distressing.

When anxiety goes unchecked for a long time, it may eventually snowball into an anxiety attack or even a full-blown panic attack.

It's completely normal to feel anxious, but, if gradually you allow yourself to become overwhelmed by anxiety, it can hinder you from really enjoying the present moment.

If our anxiety is beyond our control, then how do we deal with it? Answering that question is the purpose of this book.

This book is for anyone who is curious about mindfulness and meditation, and is interested to discover how you can develop the practice of both and bring the power of them into your day to day life.

You are not a lost cause. You can do something to change it the moment you catch yourself becoming overwhelmed with worry, having repetitive thoughts, or having feelings of tightness or nervousness coursing through your body.

Our approach is designed for individuals for whom structured programs and being ordered around, simply won't work.

You may believe that mindfulness is just the latest trend, or self-help tool. Perhaps you're uncertain, as to whether something as simple as this can really make a difference to your life.

What you'll discover, is that the power of mindfulness has been around for centuries. You'll learn about the proven techniques for managing and reducing anxiety.

You'll see how developing mindfulness and incorporating meditation into your life can help you overcome anxiety.

You'll discover proven tools and exercises to help you manage your anxiety.

Better still, you can start to see a difference in just a few days, with even bigger changes taking place over the space of a few weeks.

Let's begin!

WHAT ARE MINDFULNESS AND MEDITATION?

WHAT IS MINDFULNESS?

Mindfulness is the skill of being purposefully mindful of one's experience, as it unfolds—without the superimposition of our typical commentary and without conceptualizing.

The ability to be mindful provides a healthy way to respond to our experiences and helps us conquer the unskillful tendencies of the mind, that cause us to suffer needlessly.

The practice of meditation is the fundamental technique for the development of mindfulness. Meditation is a type of physical and mental exercise, that serves to strengthen the natural ability, to bring a perpetual awareness to our lives.

Since mindfulness is the skill of personal transparency to reality without prejudice, it is expedient that we approach the act of meditation in this vein, letting go of former expectations, ideas and opinions we may have formed about this subject. It is also essential to provide both a physical and metaphysical context helpful to meditation.

Over time, the practice of mindfulness reveals and helps to build up the qualities of wisdom and empathy, the twin virtues of discipline. Wisdom involves the ability to see clearly into the basic nature of reality.

Through meditative practice, we can profoundly perceive the eternal arising and disappearing of all phenomena and behold the inadequate quality of ordinary human experience that is obtained from the illusion of the self as an entity existing separately from the rest of reality.

The key to mindfulness is practice. Anyone can develop and apply mindfulness techniques to the simple aspects of living, such as breathing, sensing, feeling, eating, walking, talking, and even driving.

WHAT IS MEDITATION?

An incredible thing about meditation is that it is quite straightforward. All you simply have to do is to sit down, be calm, turn your attention inward, and get your mind focused. It's as simple as that.

You may be wondering why people compose such a significant number of brochures and hardcovers about meditation—including detailed work, like the one you're currently reading. Why not simply offer a couple of brief instructions and disregard all the verbiage?

Let's assume that you're planning to take a road trip to some picturesque location. You could simply scribble down the directions and follow them, one after the other. Given a couple of days, you'd likely get where you want to go.

But, there's a better chance that you'll be more likely to enjoy the trip, if you have a travel guide to point out beautiful scenery along the way.

Additionally, you may feel more secure if you carry a self-help manual to guide you through, in the event that your vehicle develops a fault. You may even like to take some side trips to scenic spots or alter your schedule completely and get there via another route, or even another vehicle!

Similarly, you can view the act of meditation to be a journey of sorts. Meditation is the act of putting your complete concentration on a particular object.

It could be something simple like a word or phrase, the flame from a candle placed on a votive holder, or a solid shape, or the rhythm of your breath.

Every day, your mind processes a barrage of sensations, ranging from visual impressions, to emotions and thoughts. When you meditate, your attention is streamlined, which, in turn, limits the stimuli bombarding your sensory nerves and, ultimately, calms your mind in the process.

Meditation helps to transform the mind. The techniques involved in meditation encourages and develops attention, certainty, emotional intelligence, and a calm observance of the original mode of things.

By getting engaged with a particular meditation practice, you become familiar with the patterns and habits of your mind. The practice offers a means to cultivate newer and more positive habits.

With constant work and patience, these nourishing, focused states of mind can transcend into a profoundly peaceful and healthy state of mind. Such experiences can bring about a complete change and can help in understanding life better.

Countless meditation practices have been developed over the centuries. They may all be referred to as 'mind-trainings', and although they adopt a wide range of approaches, the adaptation of a tranquil and optimistic state of mind, forms the basis of all of them.

Asides from mindful meditation, other forms of meditations include loving-kindness meditation, breath awareness meditation, heart rhythm meditation (HRM) and guided meditation.

2

MINDFULNESS & MEDITATION FOR ANXIETY

The art of mindfulness and meditation has been in existence for many years, but has only recently gained wider interest.

This ancient practice is equally being used by other professionals, especially in the tech world, to improve leadership skills, collaboration levels, and to reduce the cost of healthcare.

There is an increasing number of businesses that focus on teaching the various tools practiced in mindfulness and meditation, for improved focus/concentration, emotional balance, and their many other scientifically proven benefits.

Some of these companies include well-known names, such as Google, Salesforce, Aetna, Goldman Sachs Group, Blackrock, and the Bank of America.

Let's have a look at how these practices can change the wiring and makeup of our brains.

MINDFULNESS CAN REDUCE ANXIETY

A study was carried out in Massachusetts General Hospital in 2013. Ninety-three people, who had been diagnosed with a generalized anxiety disorder, were randomly allocated to two groups. Some were allocated to an 8-week group involved in a mindfulness-based stress reduction (MBSR) program, the others to a control group of stress management education (SME). The research concluded that those that belong to the MBSR group showed a significant reduction in anxiety.

MINDFULNESS CAN IMPROVE SLEEP

A study compared two meditation programs, which were centered on mindfulness, by forming two groups and then randomly distributing each study subject into one of the two groups.

One of these two groups were allowed to practice meditation, while the other group was exempt from meditation. The subjects who were allowed to meditate fell asleep sooner and stayed asleep for longer, than the other group who did not practice meditation.

The reason this works could be that the disturbing and "runaway" thoughts that often lead to sleeplessness can be redirected and managed by meditation skills.

Not only does meditation help to prevent sleeplessness, but it can also help relax the body, loosen up and release built-up tension while placing you in a peaceful state in which you're more likely to fall asleep.

MINDFULNESS MEDITATION DECREASES IMPLICIT AGE AND RACE BIAS

Humans instinctively depend on the established mental connection between ideas, as well as shortcuts to meander through life.

Shortcuts may sometimes be necessary—for instance, having a personal appeal toward what you want to eat at breakfast which may not necessarily appeal to others. This personal appeal or interest is also referred to as a bias.

Certain biases can be beneficial, albeit such is not always the case especially when it comes to the subject of age and race.

In the context of criminal law, for instance, it is essential that everybody involved in the system, from police officers to prosecutors, and defense attorneys to the judges, are mindful of their own biases.

Prof Adam Lueke of Central Michigan University, conducted a study[1] in 2015 where the participants were made to listen to either a mindfulness or a control audio.

In this investigation, mindfulness meditation caused an expansion in state mindfulness and a decline in an implied bias, in people of different color and maturity.

Professor Lueke observed that, the result was not based on the fact that the mindful group was able to detect their tendencies to be biased and, as such, were able to override it, but rather because, compared to the control group, they simply had no inclination towards being biased to start with.

Professor Lueke carried out a follow-up study, in which he went further to determine if the same mindfulness interference could affect the perceptive behavior as well.

The study subjects were made to play a game that measured their level of trust. Basically, they were made to look at a series of pictures of people from different races. Then, they were asked to select those they believed to be able to help them win money and those who were likely to rob them.

The control group appeared to trust white partners more than they trusted those who were black. On the other hand, the mindfulness group trusted both white and black people alike.

Whilst this may not apply directly to the issue of anxiety, it shows that mindfulness has the power to liberate our brains from traditional ways of thinking, and help us establish new thought patterns.

MINDFULNESS-BASED COGNITIVE THERAPY (MBCT) MAY PREVENT AND TREAT DEPRESSION

Our minds are always busy, recounting stories, translating our experience by filling in missing snippets of information, and afterward, ruminating over the stories it has created, whether they are actually true or false.

Mindfulness-Based Stress Reduction (MBSR) was originally developed as an eight-week program by Jon Kabat-Zinn in 1979.

In one study, MBSR was shown to reduce anxiety levels by up to 58% and stress by 40%.

Cognitive Behavioural Therapy (CBT) focuses on changing your thoughts and beliefs, which then impacts how you feel and act.

In one study[2], CBT was shown have a significant, positive effect for individuals with generalized anxiety disorder, depression, obsessive compulsive disorder (OCD), social phobia, post-traumatic stress disorder (PTSD) and anxiety disorders.

Mindfulness-based cognitive therapy (MBCT) is a combination of components from mindfulness-based stress reduction (MBSR) and cognitive behavioral therapy (CBT).

As mentioned by the American Psychological Association, mindfulness-based cognitive therapy is an eight-week, group-based program that uses mindfulness exercises, like yoga and body awareness.

The daily homework involves giving full attention to any task at hand, varying from doing dishes and mowing the lawn to other household chores.

According to Willem Kuyken, Ph.D., a professor at the University of Oxford in the United Kingdom, people who entertain a lot of negative thoughts, sentiments and wrong beliefs about themselves, are at greater risk of depression.

MBCT helps them to recognize this. It allows them to engage with their negative emotions in a different way and respond to it with calmness and compassion.

Professor Kuyken conducted a study which showed that MBCT helps to prevent depression recurrence just as effectively as antidepressant medication would.

MINDFULNESS MEDITATION CAN DECREASE BLOOD PRESSURE

Mindfulness meditation can equally enhance your physical wellbeing by reducing strain on the heart.

Prolonged high blood pressure ultimately results in poor heart function as it causes the heart to work harder to pump blood. Furthermore, high blood pressure may cause the arteries to narrow, a condition called atherosclerosis, which can ultimately lead to a heart attack or stroke.

In one study of 996 volunteers, the aim was to find out the effects of meditation on blood pressure. Each of the volunteers found that when they meditated by concentrating on a "silent mantra"—a repeated, non-vocalized word—their blood pressure reduced by approximately 5 points.

This was more effective among older volunteers and those who had higher blood pressure, prior to the study.

A survey revealed that there are several other types of meditation techniques which produce similar improvements in blood pressure.

Meditation appears to control circulatory strain, by relaxing the nerve signals that control heart function, tension in blood vessels, and the adrenaline responses that increase alertness in stressful situations.

Whilst not directly related to anxiety, you're beginning to see how something as seemingly simple meditation can significantly impact your wellbeing.

MINDFULNESS MEDITATION IMPROVES COGNITION AND MOOD

A study was conducted in 2010[3] and subsequently published in the Consciousness and Cognition Journal. The study included two groups: the intervention group and the control group. 24 people were assigned to the intervention group and 25 people were assigned to the control group.

The intervention group received four sessions of mindfulness meditation training, while the control group listened to an audiobook.

In the results, both the mindfulness meditation training group and the control group showed improved mood.

However, the results also showed that only meditation training reduced tiredness and anxiety, and increased mindfulness.

It was also observed, that those who underwent mindfulness training, showed improved visuospatial processing, excellent memory and executive functioning.

The conclusion made by the researchers, was that just "four days of meditation training can enhance the ability to sustain attention; benefits that have formerly been reported among long-term meditators."

That's some pretty impressive results to see after just a few days!

MINDFULNESS MEDITATION HELP THE BRAIN REDUCE DISTRACTIONS

Our mental focus is being pulled in a thousand directions at the same time. As a result, it's getting harder to teach our minds to pay complete attention to the world around us.

In one study carried out at Harvard, it was reported that "brain cells are able to regulate the flow of information, much the same way that radio stations broadcast information, through the use of particular frequencies or waves.

The alpha rhythm frequency is particularly active in the cells that coordinate touch, sight, and sound in the brain cortex, where it helps to suppress insignificant or distracting sensations and regulate the flow of sensory information between brain regions."

In this study, participants were involved in an eight-week mindfulness training program.

At the end of the program, it was observed that the control group that failed to complete the mindfulness meditation, displayed poorer and significantly less pronounced attention-based adjustments to the alpha rhythm, compared to those who had successfully completed the mindfulness meditation training.

It seems that mindfulness training can help the brain to reduce distractions, enabling us to pay attention and focus better.

THE HARDEST THING ABOUT MINDFULNESS AND MEDITATION

More than ever, learning the basics of mindfulness and meditation is hardly a difficult thing, now that there are courses, books, apps and videos that are easily accessible to anyone.

In fact, it's almost too simple. Just by spending a few minutes each day, you really can have a massive impact on your life.

Yes, of course, it isn't that simple. The benefit of mindfulness and meditation is in the repetitive nature of them, of doing them regularly, every day.

The hardest part of mindfulness and meditation is to cultivate a daily habit of it.

It's not like we can go to the gym, as we do when we want to create a habit for exercise.

Instead, we have to develop habits that can be sustained for weeks, or even months.

Just like other good habits, such as exercising and maintaining a healthy diet, it does no good to have knowledge of the benefits that may be derived from them, if one does not actually engage in them.

ACTION POINT

When can you find ten to fifteen minutes in your day, just to make a start on developing a new habit?

If you can't find ten minutes during the day, perhaps you could find time at the end of your day, to incorporate a guided meditation to help you relax and to promote a better quality of sleep?

---

1. https://journals.sagepub.com/doi/abs/10.1177/1948550614559651
2. https://www.sciencedirect.com/science/article/pii/S0272735805001005
3. https://www.sciencedirect.com/science/article/pii/S1053810010000681

MEDITATION IN PRACTICE

Mastering our thoughts has never been easy. It doesn't help that our multitasking, sensory-bombarding world makes it incredibly more difficult to master our thoughts.

However, if we are able to align our thoughts through meditation, then we will be on our way to long-life, happiness, and a good quality of physical and mental health.

Meditation is not rocket science, but that's not to say it is entirely easy either.

Meditation can help when you shift attention away from your thoughts and into your physical rhythms, like breathing. Leave the thoughts and, instead, allow yourself to just feel.

This is more powerful than it sounds, altering your physical, psychological, and emotional responses.

The following are three meditation techniques that you may find helpful.

PRACTICING RELAXATION

Herbert Benson MD, a professor at Harvard, developed a relaxation exercise in 1970. This exercise was centered on a study about the benefits of meditation.

It is called the Relaxation Response. This exercise has been demonstrated to have benefits, such as reducing stress levels, as well as other positive effects, that can be derived from relaxation.

Practicing the Relaxation Response for 15-20 minutes a day can help to reduce your stress levels significantly.

- Sit quietly in a place where you won't be disturbed.
- The process may take a while, so for more effectiveness, make yourself comfortable for the entire process. Make sure you're warm enough and won't be disturbed.
- Now that you are comfortable, proceed to choose an object to focus on. This object may be a visual symbol, for example, a solid shape. It could also be a special syllable, word or phrase, which you repeat over and over. Objects with a deep, personal or spiritual meaning are especially effective. Do everything to keep your attention focused on this object; when you get distracted, allow yourself to focus again. If your object of focus is within, then keep your eyes closed.
- Keep a responsive state of mind. Allow thoughts, images, and feelings to pass through. Don't try to hold them back and don't try to translate them either. Just let them flow freely. You may be tempted to assess your progress. Make sure you don't; just tenderly bring your attention back to focus whenever it wanders.

As you keep up this exercise regularly, you'll begin to experience the benefits of meditation.

You may notice how your body is more relaxed and your mind is more at peace.

WALKING MEDITATION

A walking meditation, which is the simplest form of moving meditation, is easy to incorporate into your day. A walking meditation can be practiced anywhere, at any time.

You might find it difficult to sit still or suffer from anxiety attacks that worsen when sitting quietly. If this is the case, a walking meditation might be the most effective method of meditation, compared to relaxation meditation.

The fact that it is termed 'walking meditation' does not mean it's the same thing as simply taking a walk. It requires deliberate attention and concentration, which is what makes it different from a simple stroll.

You can't say you're practicing a walking meditation while you're at the same time making a phone call or listening to something on a tablet. It does not work that way!

You need to consciously put one foot in front of the other, align your focus on the universe. As you take each step, let the wind caress your skin and feel the ground beneath you—now, that is a walking meditation.

If you have a maze nearby, then count yourself lucky, because doing a maze-walk is an awesome way to perform walking meditation.

In as much the same way as when you're doing a relaxation meditation, you need to gently discard any unwanted thoughts that you may encounter, as you're walking.

Remember the popular "wax on, wax off" scene in the Karate Kid movie, where a simple act of polishing a car was turned into a moving meditation?

Perhaps you can now see how almost any activity can become a meditation. The simple key to this is "mindfulness."

GUIDED MEDITATION

For complete beginners, using a guided meditation can help you develop the habit of meditation.

Listening to a guided mediation is a great way to get started, all you need to do is find a quiet place to sit or lie down, and listen.

Just a few minutes of guided meditation can help your mind begin to declutter itself from the day. It promotes relaxation, at a deep level, both physically and mentally.

As you meditate, it will slow down your brain waves and reduce your level of stress.

It's a great way to develop your creative right brain. It also calms the adrenals, stopping them from over-producing cortisol—the stress hormone.

If you're wondering what a guided meditation is, a guided meditation often includes a physical relaxation for the body, as well as a mind journey, filled with visual imagery to relax the mind.

The great thing is that you don't even need to know how to meditate, to get all the benefits! You can just listen to a meditation, to get started at any time.

4

MINDFULNESS IN PRACTICE

Do you ever get upset and annoyed with yourself for feeling disturbed, edgy or panicky? Do you respond to your frustrations by trying to resist these feelings?

If that sounds familiar, you'll soon realize that you are only strengthening these negative emotions and making them worse than they already are.

But what should you do, instead of resisting your feelings?

Mindfulness suggests you simply allow yourself to feel the way you are feeling. Learning to accept your feelings will help a great deal and they will eventually settle down or pass.

In this chapter, we'll look at some easy mindfulness techniques you can learn.

When you're faced with worry, anxiety, or a panic attack, use one of these techniques to help release your feelings and prevent them escalating.

BREATH COUNTING

This method can either be utilized in conjunction with anchoring or utilized alone.

1. The first step is anchoring. Count up to 6, as you inhale deeply, as you breathe in.
2. Then count up to 10, as you exhale.

This method has the impact of protracting both the in-breath and the out-breath, thereby slowing down your breathing.

It additionally lengthens the out-breath more than the in-breath, driving you to discharge more carbon dioxide, slowing your pulse, calming you down, and re-establishing emotional equilibrium.

Ensure you fit the numbers to your breath, and not the other way around.

On the off chance that the numbers 6 and 10 don't work for you, discover another proportion that works, provided that the out-breath is longer than the in-breath, with a minimum of two counts.

If it becomes too difficult to continue breathing at the same time as counting, you can count for one full breath, then take one normal breath and count the next one.

In the event that you can't manage counting because you're feeling anxious, here's another method. As you breathe in, say to yourself, "in", and as you breathe out, say, "out" completely, endeavoring to extend the out-breath.

Repeat the process for at least one minute, or you can go for whatever length of time that you need.

This technique can be used very effectively to ward off impending panic attacks, whether they happen in the middle of the night or during the day.

ANCHORING

One of the best ways to quiet yourself down is to ground yourself. Yes, ground yourself. In other words "anchor yourself."

You can achieve this by focusing your thoughts and attention to the lower half of your body.

- To begin, focus your attention on your feet. Concentrate on how they feel inside your socks or shoes. Pay attention to the hardness of the ground against them.
- Now that you have a complete focus on your feet, allow that focus to move from your lower legs and gradually through your upper legs. Savor the sensation. How does it feel? Dense or feathery? Toasty or chilly? Excited or paralyzed?
- To conclude the process, feel yourself inhale and exhale, and relax as you continue the breathing process.

This is an extraordinary method of anchoring yourself.

It is another method that you can practice at any time, with your eyes open or closed, in a seated position or even while moving around. It is easy to use, simply anchor yourself and then breathe.

FINGER BREATHING

Finger breathing is another adaptation of breath counting. It involves tracing around your outstretched hand.

It's a simple idea, which is visual and tactile. It's something that children and young people find easy to learn.

- Bring one of your hands in front of you with the palm facing towards you.
- Follow up the outside length of your thumb with the index finger of your other hand while you inhale. Pause at the

highest point of your thumb and then trace it down the other side while you exhale. That is one breath.

- Follow up the side of the next finger while you inhale. Pause at the top and, afterward, trace down the other side of that finger, while you exhale. That's two breaths.
- Continue tracing along each finger as you count every breath. Move back up the last finger after getting to the end of the finger and repeat the process in reverse.

This exercise is extremely valuable when there is a lot going on around you, and it's difficult to close your eyes and focus inwards.

It gives you something visual to focus on, something kinesthetic to do with your hands, and it also helps you focus on your counting and breathing.

Once you've done it once, it's also very easy to remember.

DOODLING

Yes, doodling really can have benefits beyond giving you something to do when you're bored!

Doodling is an incredible tool to activate and develop your creative self. When combined with the power of Mandala, it can help you access profound parts of your brain.

Here's an idea of how to get started:

- Draw a dot at the center of your canvas/paper. This dot represents the seed of an idea you want to expand on and get innovative with. Everything creative started from a basic seed. It's like the big bang.
- Next, you develop your idea and your creativity by drawing 4 lines out from the dot, each line pointing toward north, south, east, and west respectively.
- Continue expanding your idea by drawing the next 4 lines

out from the dot, which will look like lines extending NE, SE, SW, and NW.

- Draw a petal on each line. The petals represent your personal, creative development.
- Draw a heart in the middle of each petal and a circle around the lines.
- Then draw a heart in between every two petals
- Now draw a circle around the entire center. This speaks to advance creativity and growth, within the circles you have made, with the networks and connections you have framed.
- Draw a dot that connects each line with the circle, then, on the circle, draw 8 dots. This depicts co-creation within your connections and networks and planting seeds of growth along the way.
- Draw the image for the lotus petal, joining each dots.
- Inside each lotus petal, make a sketch of any preferred symbol. Make a sketch of a symbol that represents something significant to you, such as a flower, a musical note, or maybe a football, inside the lotus flower.
- What you doodle doesn't matter. Make a doodle of anything that comes to your mind. That's your mandala!

There is no restriction on how big or how much you draw, so you can keep expanding out and including details.

Bear in mind, however, that while it won't be perfect, it will be unique and creative!

COLORING

As a way to de-stress from our hectic lives, adult coloring books have seen a surge in popularity.

Coloring has similar benefits to doodling.

Here's one idea of how to get started:

- Keep it simple. Start with an empty page and a pencil.
- Start with a shape that you find easy to draw. For example, a circle. Remember to keep it simple.
- Draw shape after shape, and trust your gut. Perhaps create a bunch of circles together.
- If you feel there ought to be a few lines, go ahead. Make those lines. Go crazy!
- Give yourself permission to put anything on the page. You can fill the page as far as possible, or stop, when you have a craving for halting. Simply stay with it until you feel you're done.
- Go on with your day feeling invigorated. The simple act of drawing on a page and expressing your creativity can do wonders.

The most vital thing is to calm your mind.

In the event that you find yourself getting tense and worrying that you aren't doing it right, simply take a deep breath and let that self-criticism go.

The objective is to achieve a relaxed state, where you are simply giving your hand a chance to make marks on the page, and your mind to have consideration, without judgment while you aren't really thinking about anything in particular.

NOTHING NEW UNDER THE SUN

These mindfulness techniques are not new, but they do work. They have been utilized by psychologists and counselors for many years.

The fact that we can all benefit from these techniques, and the fact that they are so effective for everyday experiences, is a relatively new discovery.

Which of these mindfulness techniques will you put into practice first?

5

THE POWER OF MINDFULNESS AND MEDITATION

We live in an era of distraction. However, one of life's greatest enigmas is that your ability to focus on the present determines your brightest future.

Life unfurls in the present, yet so frequently we allow the present to slip away, misusing the valuable seconds of our lives and enabling time to surge past, unseized and imperceptible, as we ruminate about the past and worry about the future.

We're always busy, allowing little time to practice calm and stillness. We daydream about being on vacation when we're at work and, when we're on vacation, we worry about the work heaping up on our desks. We harp on obtrusive memories of the past or worry about what may or may not happen in the future.

We don't live in the present on the grounds that our "monkey minds," as Buddhists call them, jump from thought to thought, like monkeys hopping from tree to tree.

Most of us are not in control of our thoughts, rather our thoughts are in control of us.

Ordinary thoughts run through our minds like deafening cascades. In order to keep a tight rein on our lives and minds, we need to quit "doing," so we can discover the sense of balance that eludes us and focus on simply existing.

There is a need for us to live more 'in the moment'.

Living in the present, which can also be referred to as mindfulness, is the process of deliberately bringing one's attention to experiences occurring in the present moment.

When you become mindful, you become an observer of your thoughts from moment to moment, without making decisions about them.

Mindfulness is to do with leaving your thoughts as they are, neither pushing them away nor grasping at them. It also involves an awakening to experience, rather than letting your life go by without living it.

Living in the moment involves a profound enigma: You can't pursue it for its advantages, you just have to believe that the reward will come. Pursuing mindfulness for its advantages only propels a future-oriented mindset, which will ruin the entire idea.

There are numerous paths to mindfulness and at the center of each is a paradox.

Ironically, letting go of what you want is the only way to get it.

Here are some tricks to help you...

UNSELFCONSCIOUSNESS

To enhance your efficiency, stop thinking about it

I have never been comfortable on a dance floor. My movement feels awkward. I never figured out what to do with my arms. I feel like people are making fun of me. I can't let go because I know I look ludicrous.

People always said, "Free yourself. Nobody's watching you. Everyone's too busy worrying about themselves." but that never rung true for me. If that's true, then how come they always make fun of my moves?

The term "absolute beginner" is what the dance world uses to describe people like me. That is why Jessica, the owner of a dance studio in Manhattan, started from scratch by having me sit on a bench and making me tap my feet to the beat as Jay-Z pounded away in the background.

We spent whatever was left of the class moving just our shoulders, ribs, or hips, in order to build body awareness, an activity referred to as "isolations."

"Present-moment awareness was more vital than body awareness," Jessica said. "Be right here, right now! Simply let go and let yourself be in the moment," she added.

Thinking too much about what you're doing will only make you worse. That's the first enigma of living in the present. Whenever I say, 'be here with me now,' all I'm saying is, do not get too 'in-your-head' or zone out. Rather, follow my vitality, my movements," says Jessica.

If you happen to be in a situation that makes you anxious, such as giving a discourse, acquainting yourself with a stranger, or dancing, focusing on your anxiety will only increase it.

So, focus less on what's going on in your mind and more on what's happening in the room. Less on your mental babble and more on yourself, as an integral component of something.

In order to be more of myself, I needed to shift my focus from myself to some outside-myself things, like the music or the people around me.

When people are mindful, they're bound to experience themselves as part of humanity, as a component of a greater universe. Certainly, mindfulness obscures the line between self and other. That's the reason profoundly mindful individuals, such as Buddhist monks, talk about being "at one with everything."

"Mindfulness helps reduce self-consciousness, thereby enabling you to witness the passing show of emotions, social pressures, even of being respected or derided by others without taking their assessments to heart," explained K. W. Brown and Richard Ryan of the University of Rochester.

Focusing on your immediate experience without attaching it to your self-esteem will make unpleasant events, like social rejection or your supposed friends making fun of your dancing, seem less threatening.

"Being present-minded takes away some of that self-assessment and getting lost in your mind, because the mind is where we make the assessments that torture us," says Stephen Schueller, an assistant professor at the University of California, Irvine.

So, focusing on the present moment drives you to stop overthinking and sets you free, rather than getting stuck in your head and worrying.

SAVORING

To abstain from worrying about the future, concentrate on the present

Elizabeth Gilbert, in her autobiography titled "Eat, Pray, Love", wrote about a friend who, in a near panic, exclaims whenever she sees a beautiful place, "It's so beautiful here! Someday, I want to come back here!"

Gilbert states that it takes all her persuasive powers to try to convince her that she is already here.

We're so often trapped in thoughts of the past or the future that we forget to experience, let alone enjoy, what is happening right now.

We sip espresso and think, "This isn't as good as what I had a week ago." We eat a biscuit and we think, "I hope I don't exhaust all my biscuits."

Revel or relish in whatever you're doing at the present moment. This is what psychologists call *savoring*.

"This could be while you're taking a shower, eating a cake or basking in the sun. You could be savoring a win or savoring music. Savoring usually involves your senses," explains Sonja Lyubomirsky, the author of The How of Happiness, who also happens to be a psychologist at the University of California, Riverside.

When you take a couple of minutes, each day, to effectively savor something you usually rush through, such as drinking a cup of tea, eating a meal, or strolling to the bus, you'll find yourself experiencing more delight, bliss, and other positive emotions and fewer depressive symptoms.

Due to the fact that most negative thoughts concern the past or the future, living in the moment makes people more joyful, not just at the moment they are tasting molten chocolate pooling on their tongues, but lastingly.

The hallmark of anxiety and depression is worrying about something that has not occurred yet and might not occur by any means.

As Mark Twain stated, "I have known a great many troubles, but most of them never happened."

Worry means thinking about the future. So, when you lift yourself into awareness of the present moment, worry melts away.

The other side of anxiety is ruminating, which involves thinking bleakly about events in the past. Ruminating stops the moment you shift your focus into the present, which can only be achieved by savoring.

Savoring forces you into the present and prevents you from feeling anxious about things that aren't happening at the moment.

BREATHE

In the event that you need a future with your life partner, inhabit the present

Living consciously, with keen interest, can powerfully affect interpersonal life.

Mindfulness actually immunizes individuals against aggressive impulses, says Whitney Heppner and Michael Kernis of the University of Georgia.

In one of their studies, a subject was informed that other subjects were forming a group and that they were taking a vote on whether that person could join. Five minutes later, the experimenter declared the outcome of whether the subject had been rejected or accepted.

Before the study, half of the subjects had undergone a mindfulness activity in which each slowly ate a raisin, focusing on every sensation and savoring its flavor and texture.

Afterward, in what they thought was a different test, subjects had the chance to convey a painful blast of noise to someone else. Among subjects who didn't participate in the exercise of eating the raisin, those who heard that the group had rejected them became aggressive, and they took it out on other people by inflicting long and painful sonic blasts, seemingly without provocation.

However, it did not matter to those who'd eaten the raisin first, whether they'd been rejected or embraced. Either way, they were unwilling to inflict pain on others. They were as serene as those who were given a word of social acceptance.

"Mindfulness decreases ego involvement," explains Kernis. "So, people are more likely to take things literally and are less likely to link their self-esteem to events."

Mindfulness can also make people feel more connected to each other, this includes the empathic sensation of being "at one with the universe."

It helps you decipher and respond to what's going on in your mind. It expands the gap between emotional impulse and action, enabling you to do what Buddhists call "recognizing the spark before the flame."

Focusing on the present reboots your mind, enabling you to respond keenly, rather than automatically. Instead of backing down in fear, lashing out in anger, or mindlessly following a passing hankering, you get the chance to say to yourself, "This is the emotion I'm feeling. How should I respond?"

Since you're not becoming deregulated by attacks to your self-esteem, you're better able to regulate your behavior. That's the other incongruity: Inhabiting your own mind more fully has a powerful effect on your interactions with others. Thus, mindfulness increases self-control.

It is quite impractical to dodge out and savor a raisin, amid a flare-up with your partner. However, breathing is a basic exercise you can do anywhere, anytime, to initiate mindfulness.

It turns out that, the advice my friend received in the desert one time was accurate: There's no better way to carry yourself into the present moment, than to focus on your breathing.

Setting your awareness on what's happening at the moment pushes you forcefully into the present moment.

For many, a preferred method of orienting themselves into the present moment is focusing on the breath, not on the grounds that the breath has some enchanting property, but because it's always there with you.

FLOW

To take advantage of time, forget about it

Maybe the complete way of living in the moment is the state of total absorption, referred to by psychologists as "flow."

Flow occurs when you're so preoccupied in a task that you forget about everything else around you. Flow includes an apparent incongruity: How can you be living in the moment, if you're not even aware of the moment?

The profundity of commitment absorbs you powerfully by keeping attention so focused that distractions cannot find the way in.

You focus and get so engrossed in what you're doing that you're oblivious to the passage of time. Hours can go by without you realizing it.

Flow, as with romance or sleep, is a slippery state in which you can't simply will yourself into. All you can do is to create the ideal conditions for it to happen.

The primary prerequisite for flow is to set an objective that's difficult, however, not unattainable. Something for which you have to marshal your assets and stretch yourself to accomplish.

The undertaking should be matched to your ability level; it should not be so difficult that you'll feel stressed, and not so easy that you'll get exhausted.

In a state of flow, you're firing on all cylinders to rise to a challenge.

To set the phase for flow, objectives need to be clearly stated, with the goal of knowing your succeeding step.

"It could be playing at the next bar in a list of music, turning the page if you're perusing a decent novel or finding the next foothold, if you happen to be a rock climber, and at the same time you're somewhat anticipating," says Mihaly Csikszentmihalyi, the psychologist who first defined the concept of flow.

The task should be set up in such a way that you get direct and immediate feedback, with your successes and failures evident. Just as a climber on the mountain knows immediately if their foothold is secure, and a pianist knows instantly when they've played the wrong note, you can seamlessly adjust your conduct.

Self-consciousness dissipates, as your attention focus narrows.

You feel as though your awareness merges with the activity you're performing and you feel a sense of personal dominion over the circumstance; the exercise is basically rewarding that, despite the fact that the task is difficult, the action feels easy.

ACCEPTANCE

If something is pestering you, move toward it rather than far from it

We all experience pain in our lives, be it the sudden rush of anxiety when we get up to give a discourse, the ex we still long for, or the jackhammer growling across the street.

If we give them a chance, such irritants can divert our attention from the enjoyment of life. "Paradoxically, the undeniable reaction of focusing on the problem, with the goal of battling and overcoming it, often makes it worse," argues Steven C. Hayes, a psychologist at the University of Nevada.

The mind's natural inclination, when faced with pain, is to endeavor to avoid it by trying to oppose unpleasant thoughts, emotions and sensations.

For instance, when we lose in love, we battle with the feelings of heartbreak. While waiting for a painful root canal when we're sitting in the dentist's chair, we wish we didn't have to go there. As we grow older, we wish we were younger.

However, most of the time, negative feelings and circumstances can't be avoided, and opposing them only amplifies the pain.

The problem is that we don't just have primary emotions, but we also have emotions about other emotions, which is referred to as secondary emotions.

We get worried and then think, "I wish I weren't so worried." For example, if the primary emotion has to do with worry over your workload. The secondary emotion is an emotion about another emotion, for example, "I detest being worried."

The solution to this problem is acceptance. It involves giving the emotion the chance to be there.

In other words, being comfortable with the way things are in every moment, without endeavoring to manipulate or change the experience, without judging it, clinging to it, or pushing it away. Attempting to change it only frustrates and drains you. Acceptance mitigates you of this unnecessary extra suffering.

Let's assume you've just broken up with your partner and you're feeling heartbroken. You could endeavor to battle these emotions by saying, "I hate feeling this way; I have to make this feeling go away."

Focusing on the pain, that is, being miserable about being sad, will only prolong the sadness. However, you can help yourself out by accepting your feelings instead, by saying, "I've just had a breakup. Feelings of loss are typical and natural. It's all right for me to feel like this."

The fact that you accepted an unpleasant situation doesn't mean you don't have objectives for the future. It only means you acknowledge that certain things are beyond your control and that the outrage, stress, sadness, or pain is there, in any case. So, it is better to embrace the feeling, as it is.

Acceptance of the present moment isn't the same thing as acquiescence, and it doesn't mean that you have to like what's happening. It doesn't show you what to do, neither does it reveal what happens next, that has to come out of your comprehension of the current moment.

In the event that you feel anxious, for example, you can accept the feeling, label it as anxiety and then direct your attention to something else instead. You watch your thoughts, perceptions, and emotions flutter through your mind without taking part.

Thoughts are simply thoughts. You don't need to trust them or believe what they say.

ENGAGEMENT

Understand that you are clueless

It's very possible that you've had the experience of driving along a highway, only to suddenly realize that you zoned out and that you have no memory or awareness of the previous 15 minutes.

Perhaps you even missed your exit and it's as if you've suddenly woken up at the wheel. Or maybe it happens when you're perusing a book, and you've said to yourself, "I know I just perused that page, but I have no clue what it said."

These autopilot moments, when you're so lost in your thoughts that you aren't aware of your present experience, are called mindlessness.

Accordingly, life passes you by without enlisting you. According to

Prof Ellen Langer, a professor of psychology at Harvard University, the most ideal approach to evade such blackouts is to develop the tendency of always noticing new things in whatever circumstances you find yourself in.

That process makes engagement with the present moment and has a cascade of other advantages. Noticing new things emphatically puts you in the present.

We become mindless in the light of the fact that once we think we know something, as a result, we quit focusing on it. We go about our regular drive in a haze since we've taken the same route a hundred times before.

However, if we see the world with fresh eyes, we realize almost everything is different each time. The outline of light on the buildings, the faces of the people, even the sensations and feelings we experience en-route, noticing each moment with another, fresh quality. This has been termed "beginner's mind" by some people.

"By procuring the tendency of noticing new things, we recognize that the world is actually evolving constantly. We really don't know how the coffee is going to taste or how the drive will be, or maybe we're not sure" says Professor Langer. "Orchestra musicians who are told to make their performance new in inconspicuous ways, enjoy themselves better and the audiences actually prefer those performances."

When we're present at the moment, making it new, it leaves an imprint in the things we compose, the art we create, the music we play and in all that we do.

The moment you realize that you don't know the things you've constantly underestimated, you set out of the house quite differently.

It becomes an adventure in paying attention and the more you pay attention, the more you new things you see. And the more excitement you experience.

6

CONCLUSION

Mindfulness itself is easy, but living a consistently mindful life requires effort.

> "*People make it a goal to be mindful for the next 2 weeks or the next 20 minutes ... then they think mindfulness is hard, because they have the wrong yardstick.*
>
> *The correct yardstick is just for this moment.*"

This quote is from family physician, Jay Winner, author of "Take the Stress out of Your Life."

Mindfulness is the only intentional, orderly activity that is not focused on improving yourself. It is only a matter of acknowledging where you already are.

Mindfulness was summed up by a cartoon in The New Yorker: Two monks are sitting next to each other, meditating. The more youthful one is giving the elderly one a questioning look, which prompts the older one to respond, "*Nothing takes place after this. This is it.*"

You can choose to be mindful at any moment just by focusing on what is happening at the moment. You can do it right now.

What's going on right now? Consider yourself as an eternal observer, and just observe the moment. What do you see, hear, and smell?

Regardless of how it feels, pleasant or unpleasant, good or bad, all you need to do is go with the flow, since that's what's present.

What's more, if you notice your mind wandering, bring yourself back. Simply say to yourself, "Now. Now. Now."

The principal paradox of all is that mindfulness isn't an objective, because objectives are about the future. However, you do have to set the aim of focusing on what's happening at the present moment.

As you read the words imprinted on this page, as you feel gravity securing you to the planet, as your eyes recognize the black scrawl on white paper, awaken.

Breathe, be aware of being alive. Get your focus on how your abdomen rises on the in-breath as you draw air in, the surge of warmth through your nostrils on the out-breath.

If you are paying attention to that feeling right now, as you're reading this, you're living in the moment.

Nothing happens next. It's not a journey.

This is it. You're, as of now, there.

If you want to develop your mindfulness and meditation, practice daily. Begin by committing to a timeframe that you can easily stick to, for instance, 2-10 minutes every day.

After practicing for 7 days, re-evaluate and check whether you'd jump at the chance to meditate for longer (or maybe shorter).

The most incredible verification of whether or not these practices will "work" for you is your own experience.

So make sure you give it a try and see for yourself!

ONE MORE THING

If you've enjoyed this book, please consider taking a moment to leave a rating or review.

You might also enjoy another book by the author. Paul's books are also available as audiobooks, which are free to download and listen to, if you're not already an Audible member.

CBT for Anxiety - CBT offers proven strategies and techniques for anyone suffers with anxiety, panic attacks or compulsive disorders to break free by rewiring your brain.

In this workbook, you'll learn how to:

- Identify unhelpful thought patterns and negative thoughts
- Retrain your brain to help overcome stress and anxiety
- Become calmer and more confident
- Break free from bad habits that are holding you back from living the life you want

Regain control over your life with these proven CBT techniques that you can start using today.

EMOTIONAL FREEDOM TECHNIQUES & TAPPING FOR BEGINNERS

EFT TAPPING SOLUTION MANUAL : 7 EFFECTIVE TAPPING THERAPY TECHNIQUES FOR OVERCOMING ANXIETY AND STRESS

EMOTIONAL FREEDOM
TECHNIQUES AND TAPPING
FOR BEGINNERS

**EFT TAPPING SOLUTION MANUAL : 7 EFFECTIVE TAPPING THERAPY
TECHNIQUES FOR OVERCOMING ANXIETY AND STRESS WITH
ANXIETY AND PHOBIA SCRIPTS**

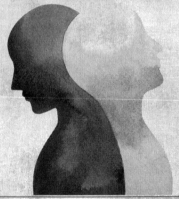

PAUL ROGERS, ROBERT BLOOM

INTRODUCTION

Our lives are filled with unprecedented levels of stress and anxiety, whether it's our job, family or money worries.

We can feel stressed, angry, struggle to meet deadlines or feel as though we have been badly treated.

These stressors, big or small, can have serious and far-reaching consequences on our lives, whether it's on our health and wellbeing, or our goals and dreams.

Of course, we know that we should deal with the stress, but we simply don't have the time or energy.

So, what's the solution to our dilemma?

Emotional Freedom Technique, also known as EFT, is something you can easily learn and integrate into your daily life.

By learning some simple tapping techniques, you'll be able to deal with stress and anxiety in a natural and effective way.

This will allow you to unshackle yourself from depression, anxiety and even some physical pain, and empower you with positive energy and motivation, so that you can live the life you've always dreamed of.

If you think this sounds all a bit too crazy to be true, let me say right now, there are several scientific papers that have validated the benefits of EFT and tapping techniques.

EFT is a holistic therapy that you can do anywhere and at any time by yourself.

It allows you to 'tap' into your body's energy and can reduce or even remove negative emotions which have a harmful impact on your health.

It combines pressing on meridian (energy) points in the body, with positive affirmations and some of the principles of meditation, which combine together in an effective three pronged attack on underlying health issues.

Peter was highly skeptical about EFT. It all sounded a bit too esoteric. However, circumstances in his life were really bad and he decided to try it, thinking 'Why not?'.

He jumped in with both feet and was committed to trying it for at least 30 days, before making any judgments. To Peter's surprise he found it hugely beneficial and effective. He still practices EFT today.

Research by the Center for Disease Control and Prevention (CDC) estimates that 85 percent of all disease is caused by negative emotions. That's an astonishing figure!

Our negative emotions release various stress hormones into our bodies, such as cortisol, that can negatively affect our immune systems. That's why having a positive attitude is crucial for our health and wellbeing.

EFT works by dealing with the emotional causes that underlie the disease or physical pain.

In today's society, too many of us are dependent upon pills to cure illness, whether it's depression or anxiety. This can often present more problems, through additional side effects and physical dependency.

One of the great things about EFT is that it is a holistic approach, where no pills are needed. It's something you can try yourself at home, you can start seeing benefits quickly, potentially saving you both time and money.

Despite it's rather scientific start, EFT has been streamlined into an easy, yet highly effective self-therapy, that anyone can use on their own.

This book includes step-by-step instructions, together with scripts for anxiety and phobias, to help guide you through the routine.

Of course, it's not intended to replace your medical program or advice from your physician, but it can be used in combination with it for greater results.

If you're ready to start your tapping journey to better health and emotional freedom, read on!

1

WHAT IS TAPPING?

Let's start by looking at just what tapping is and where the idea originated from.

EFT AND TAPPING

Emotional freedom therapy (also known as EFT) is a new psychological treatment method, an alternative therapy, which is widely practiced by people all over the world.

Research has shown that EFT is a very effective and efficient method that can help people in multiple ways. It can help treat psychological issues like stress, anxiety and overcome addictions like smoking, drinking, gambling etc. It can also be helpful in improving self-esteem and self-confidence.

EFT is based on tapping our meridian points and makes use of scripts to overcome and treat problems. You may use this powerful healing technology either by taking support from a therapist or by carrying out the techniques by yourself.

EFT is a type of energy therapy and works in a similar way to other energy therapies, such as acupuncture and acupressure. It's believed that EFT works by rebalancing energy flow as it moves across channels in your body known as meridians.

Research has shown that EFT taps into a section of the brain that stores and processes data, which is used in neurophysiology.

EFT practitioners believe that negative thoughts linger as blockages in your brain, which could result in an array of symptoms like fear, anger, stress etc. Some of the causes behind such negative emotions include psychological or emotional disturbances or events.

If you feel that you are inadequately trained, or that the trauma is too intense, or feel there is a lack of progress, then get in touch with a qualified practitioner who can help work on your issues and also offer support and advice on how to improve your own self-practice.

ORIGINS OF TAPPING

Emotional freedom therapy has its roots based on therapies like Neuro-Linguistic Programming (also known as NLP), Behavioral Kinesiology and Thought Field Therapy (also known as TFT).

There is an interesting story about the origin of Thought Field Therapy, which in turn paved the way for Emotional Freedom Therapy.

Dr. Roger Callahan was a cognitive psychologist and hypnotherapist who specialized in phobias. He was researching about Chinese meridians and their effect when you tap at certain meridian points.

A patient who was suffering from intense phobia of water, came to see Dr. Roger Callahan. He had already tried certain conventional therapies to cure her but was not successful. She complained that she often feels pain in her stomach even when she just thinks about water and her phobia.

Dr. Roger Callahan asked her to tap beneath her eyes for couple of times (this location corresponds to stomach meridian). By applying this seemingly simple technique the patient was relieved of the phobia.

Later, Gary Craig who worked with Dr. Roger Callahan in Thought Field Therapy started to apply this technique to his patients. He improved some techniques and simplified the process and this adapted method became Emotional Freedom Therapy.

2

HOW EFT WORKS

The emotional freedom technique uses acupressure and psychology to help improve a person's emotional health.

Even though emotional health tends to be overlooked, it plays a crucial part in a person's physical health and their ability to heal. It doesn't matter how devoted a person is to maintaining proper lifestyle and diet, if they have emotional barriers standing in their way, they won't achieve the body that they want.

Most of the time, you can apply EFT directly to your physical symptoms to find relief without working through the emotional contributors. However, for a powerful and lasting result, you need to figure out and work through the emotional issues.

The premise of EFT also understands that the more emotional issues you can work through, the more emotional peace and freedom you will have. With EFT you can get rid of limiting beliefs, increase personal performance, improve relationships, and have better physical health. To be honest, everybody on Earth has a couple of emotional issues that they are holding onto.

EFT is extremely easy to learn and can help you in areas such as:

achieving positive goals, eliminating or reduce pain, reduction of food cravings, and the removal of negative emotions. And that's just the beginning of what it can do for you.

EFT is based on the meridians of energy that have been used in traditional acupuncture to heal emotional and physical problems for more than five thousand years, but without using needles. Instead, it uses simple tapping of the fingertips to move kinetic energy into a specific meridian while you think about your problem and speak an affirmation.

The use of affirmations and tapping the meridians help to clear the emotional block from the bioenergy system. This then helps to restore the body and mind balance that is needed for optimal health.

There are many that are wary of this practice at first, mainly the thoughts of electromagnetic energy that flows through the body. Then are others that are taken aback by the thoughts of how EFT tapping works.

You need to understand that with this technique you will be tapping with your fingers. There are several acupuncture meridians that live on your fingertips, so when you tap, you are using the energy in your fingertips as well as the energy of the area that you are tapping.

Traditionally the tapping is performed by the index and middle finger and with one hand only. You can use whichever hand that you want. Many of the tapping points are on either side of your body, so that means you can use whichever side you want, and you can switch sides during a tapping session.

You can also modify the practice by using all of your fingers and both hands to create a gentle, natural curved line. The more fingers you use, them more acupuncture points you will access to. You will also cover more area so that you can hit the points easier than with a couple of fingers. It's also important that you take off any bracelets or watches that you may be wearing.

AFFIRMATION STATEMENTS

Another important part is coming up with the affirmation statement that you will use. Traditionally, the phrase is something like "Even thought I have this (fill in the blank), I deeply and completely accept myself."

You would fill in the blank with a short description of the negative emotion, food craving, addiction, or other problem that you are experiencing.

You can also use the following variations. All of the following are great to use because they use the same basic format. Meaning, they acknowledge what the problem is and create acceptance despite the problem's existence. Those are the things that are important in creating an effective affirmation. The traditional one is easier to remember, but feel free to use one of the following.

"I accept myself even though I (fill in the blank)," or "Even though I (fill in the blank), I profoundly and deeply accept myself."

You can also use "I accept and love myself even though I (fill in the blank)."

Some interesting facts about affirmations are:

You don't have to believe you affirmation truly; all you have to do is say it.

It's more effective if you can say it with emphasis and feeling, but just saying it will still do the job.

It's better to speak it out loud, but if you are in public where you need to mutter it or do it silently, it will be just as effective.

You can tune into your problem simply by thinking of what it is.

If you don't tune into your problem, which creates energy disruptions, then EFT will not be effective.

ADVICE AND CAUTION

You should only ever do what feels right for yours. Never enter into any physical or emotional waters that could be threatening.

It's your job to make sure you stay safe in this setting. You can easily seek professional assistance if you need to. Here is some advice before you dive into EFT.

- It is extremely important that you are super specific with your language when you use EFT
- You have to be completely tuned into your issue. Many times, if you are dealing with something that is very painful, you will try to disconnect from your feelings.
- Because you are working with energy, it is important to pay attention for a cognitive shift. You will know when one has happened because you will reframe the problem. When you see the problem from a different angle, you will likely be surprised or have a new insight. This is great when this happens, and it may open new, valuable insights.
- Make sure you stay well hydrated. Water helps to conduct electricity, and you are accessing electrical energy when practicing EFT.

EFT APPLICATION RANGE

The only thing that can limit what EFT can do for you is your imagination.

Experienced practitioners and the EFT originators all over the world, amongst them, are psychotherapists and psychologists, have used EFT on several different issues.

This means that they have used not only with emotional issues, where it works the best, but also for physical issues, with surprising success, whenever there is an emotional component or related traumatic experience.

But that's not the only thing; EFT is also a great tool to use for personal development. It can help to get rid of self-imposed restrictions that prevent people from experiencing abundance, great relationships, wealth, and happiness in their life.

In EFT's short history, it has already been able to help over a thousand people with many common emotional problems, including:

- Confusion, grief, guilt and almost any other emotion you can imagine
- Self-doubt
- Inner child issues and negative memories
- All types of phobias and fears
- Depression
- Frustration and anger
- Anxiety and stress

The amazing thing is that the benefits don't end there. EFT tapping isn't just limited to getting rid of painful emotions.

It can also help improve your health by:

- increasing feelings of wellbeing
- helping insomnia
- relieving feelings of pain
- reducing physical cravings, for example, for chocolate and cigarettes

It can improve your effectiveness in the things that you do, including:

- give you confidence to speak in front of a crowd and with the

people that you are not able to communicate with at the moment
- improve personal and business relationships
- improve your performance in sports, job, and any other areas of your life

Make your quality of life better, including by:

- encouraging spiritual and personal growth
- giving you courage to try things that you have wanted to, but were afraid to
- removing blockages that have kept you from having a life that is full of love and joy

There are many examples of people that have been able to easily recover from emotions that have bothered them for years, and sometimes decades, with the use of EFT.

It has been something that people could turn to for help when nothing else has been able to help them. It has also successfully helped reduce several physical systems such as insomnia, back pain, and headaches.

The power of EFT is at its best when the physical symptoms are also linked to anxiety and stress. The developers of EFT had reported a success rate of 80 to 100 percent when it came to emotional problems. When it comes to physical ailments, the percentage of success is somewhat lower. Most of the time, the effects of EFT are permanent and if they aren't you can easily repeat the process if needed.

It works quickly and is gentle. Often people can release emotions like stress, anger, anxiety, and fear in one session, a few days, or a couple of weeks as compared to months or years when it comes to traditional therapy.

One of the best things about EFT is the fact that it is so versatile.

When you master the skills that it takes, which aren't hard, it's almost like developing your superpowers.

You can use these tools in pretty much any situation. Like if you have a big presentation to give at work, or you're going in for a job interview, you can use EFT right before to help calm down your nervousness. It doesn't require anything special, yet it works wonders and can be used anywhere.

3

THE SCIENCE & PHILOSOPHY OF EFT TAPPING

EFT tapping is based on the centuries old Meridian System of healing pioneered by the Chinese.

Acupuncture and acupressure, which are forms of Meridian System healing, are now accepted healing techniques validated by acclaimed scientific institutions such as Harvard, Stanford, and other prominent universities and prestigious hospitals in the world.

In a way, since acupuncture and acupressure have already gained acceptance as a healing technique, then we can say so should EFT tapping. After all, EFT tapping is a form of acupressure and acupuncture being based on the Meridian System of healing as well.

If you want more evidence regarding the authenticity and effectiveness of EFT tapping you only need do a bit of research on the internet and you will find a wealth of scientific studies being conducted on EFT tapping.

In a 2012 study into the effects of EFT on stress, subjects were randomly assigned to either an emotional freedom technique (EFT) group, a psychotherapy group receiving a supportive interviews (SI), or a no treatment (NT) group.

The EFT group showed statistically significant improvements in anxiety and depression, compared with the group who received no treatment and were shown to have lower levels of the stress hormone, cortisol.

In another study, to investigate whether Thought Field Therapy (also known as TFT) could have an impact on a variety of anxiety disorders.

45 patients were assigned randomly to either TFT or a control group waiting list.

Those patients assigned to the TFT treatment group showed a significant decrease in all symptoms.

More interesting though was that the significant improvement seen after treatment was still evident on year later, showing that TFT may have an enduring anxiety-reducing effect.

A study in 2013 set out to evaluate the short-term effects of EFT on tension-type headache sufferers. Patients were randomly assigned to one of two groups. Those in the EFT group reported significantly reduced frequency and intensity of headache episodes.

It's early days for the science behind EFT, but of course, it was only a few decades ago that acupuncture and acupressure were considered as weird alternative therapies too.

If you really want to determine how useful EFT tapping is, the best way is to give it a test run and start practicing it.

You, yourself, are the best measure of how effective a healing technique EFT tapping is for your own emotional issues.

THE FIRST DISCOVERY STATEMENT: EMOTIONAL HEALING

The philosophy behind EFT tapping can be summed up in one statement:

The cause of all negative emotions is the disruption in the body's energy system.'

With EFT tapping, we do not believe that illness causing negative emotion is caused by remembering a traumatic experience in the past.

Practitioners of EFT tapping disagree with the conventional practice of psychotherapy to relieve traumatic memory again and again in order for the person to heal from their negative emotional effects.

Although EFT tapping believe it necessary to recognize the memory, in order to heal however, it is more important to identify how and where in the body the energy system was disrupted by the memory or experience.

Healing should be focused more on identifying the pressure point of the Meridian system that has been disrupted and apply EFT tapping techniques on said pressure point to get the energy flowing as it normally does.

THE SECOND DISCOVERY STATEMENT: PHYSICAL RELIEF

EFT can assist physical healing by resolving underlying energetic or emotional contributors.

EFT practitioners understand that not all physical ailments require tapping into emotional triggers in order for EFT tapping techniques to heal them. The reason for this is because some physical ailments are merely caused by a disruption to the balance of the energy flow in the system. They are not caused by emotional stress or trauma.

When this happens, healing the physical ailment will only require tapping at the particular pressure point, without focusing the mind on an emotional catalyst.

Some physical illnesses are so basic that all it requires is tapping at the point of the body where the energy circuit is located.

When using EFT tapping to heal the body, mind and spirit it is necessary to distinguish between illness that is caused by emotional stress or a mere physical disruption to the energy flow in the Meridian system of the body.

The reason for this is that EFT tapping healing techniques differ depending on the ailment. Is it caused by emotional trauma or by physical disruption to the energy flow? To be effective make sure you are able to identify between the two so that you can identify the most effective EFT tapping technique for healing.

EFT TAPPING POINTS: THE ENERGY MERIDIAN

In order to practice EFT tapping and enjoy its health benefits it is first necessary to understand the EFT tapping points or the energy meridian located all around the body.

Below you'll find a list of EFT tapping points, they are the locations of the ends of the energy meridian and are situated just underneath the skin.

These EFT tapping points are very sensitive to the touch. These same pressure points are used by acupressure and acupuncture to bring healing and physical ease to the body.

Here are the locations of the EFT tapping points:

1. The top of the head or also known as the Governing Vessel
2. The start of the eyebrow or the Bladder Meridian
3. The Sore Spot or the Neurolymphatic Point
4. The side of the eye or the Gall Bladder Meridian
5. Under the eye or the Stomach Meridian
6. Under the nose or the Governing Vessel
7. The chin or the Central Vessel

8. The start of the collar bone or the Kidney Meridian
9. Below the nipple or the Liver Meridian
10. The Karate Chop or the Small Intestine Meridian
11. The Baby Finger or the Heart Meridian
12. The Middle Finger or the Heart Protector
13. The Index Finger or the Large Intestine Meridian
14. The Thumb or the Lung Meridian
15. Under the arm or the Spleen Meridian

Each of these tapping points is connected to a specific and key organ of the body. This means that the body's organs are the energy circuit points where energy flows to in order to keep the body healthy.

It would be helpful for you to learn and memorize which organ of the body every EFT tapping point is connected to. This way, you will be able to zero in on the EFT point in order to heal the particular part of the body that is ailing.

For example, if you have a migraine, it could be beneficial to tap on the EFT points located in the head area for immediate relief.

If you are looking for complete and long term healing, it is best to cover all 15 EFT tapping points in one session. The same way a full body massage, or full body acupressure session, brings over all relief to the entire body, mind and soul, a full body EFT tapping session can have the same comprehensive easing of tension and stress throughout the body.

Some people find the below-the-nipple EFT tapping point a bit of an awkward tapping point to cover. It is alright to skip this part during your EFT tapping session. But it may come in handy when you have health issues to address that affect the Liver Meridian. When you do it is necessary to tap the below the nipple EFT tapping point.

A special EFT tapping point that is not included in the list is called the Gamut. It is located in the back of both hands and is behind & between the knuckles just at the base of the ring finger. It is an important EFT tapping point that is connected to the heart, the lungs and the liver.

Go ahead stand in front of the mirror and locate all 16 EFT tapping points. It is necessary to familiarize yourself first about where each tapping point is located. It is a good and necessary start to practicing EFT tapping techniques.

4

HOW DOES TAPPING COMPARE TO
OTHER THERAPIES?

Before we get into the detail of using EFT, let's take a quick look at some of the other therapies that relate to the emotions, health and wellbeing.

NEURO-LINGUISTIC PROGRAMMING (NLP)

Neuro-linguistic programming (also known as NLP) was developed by Richard Bandler and Dr. John Grinder in the 1970s, and is used by people all over the word for resolving both personal and business issues.

NLP is comprised of numerous techniques that affect the way you communicate with yourself and how you could potentially influence communication in others.

This therapy also teaches you how one person's negative thoughts affect them and how these thoughts could be transformed into positive ones.

As the name implies, there is a connection between the neurological process, language and behavioral patterns, which is used to bring about positive changes in life. Like EFT, this treatment is also helpful in treating problems like phobias, depression, anxiety etc.

It involves a lot of visualization if you're interested in motivation and requires you to visualize with as many of your senses as possible.

If you're having issues with anxiety then there are techniques that teach about models and how each person has a different concept of reality. There's also reframing which is a useful technique in change perspectives on certain events.

THETA HEALING

This method of treatment was created by Vianna Stibal in 1995 as a way to heal herself from a critical ailment. Theta healing is based on magnetic forces and its connection with your subconscious mind.

For instance, when someone encourages you by saying, "You have done a good job", how does it make you feel? You would most likely feel energized and motivated. This positive self-talk is one of many techniques used in theta healing.

Theta healing revolves around four key points – core beliefs, genetic, history and soul.

- *Core beliefs*: These are the beliefs that dwell in your subconscious mind from birth to the present.
- *Genetic:* This is based upon traits you have inherited from your parents and ancestors.
- *History:* This includes assurances, promises, and memories from your present or past life.
- *Soul:* Soul refers to the real you, the one that stays even after you die.

Electrical signals are produced in your brain, which is measured in the unit hertz. If you enter into theta brainwave, theta healing can occur.

Theta healing can help you to overcome emotional blocks, get rid of genetic and family patterns of beliefs and can help to heal physical ailments.

- *Beta waves* (14–20 hertz): This is regarded as the normal waking conscious level where you are performing routine activities.
- *Alpha waves* (8–13 hertz): This is regarded as a state of light meditation and it is similar to daydreaming.
- *Theta waves* (4–7 hertz): This is regarded as a state of creativity or is similar to a deep meditative state. This is the level that you would be when you are performing theta healing.
- *Delta waves* (1.5–3 hertz): In this wave level, you would be in a deep sleep, unconscious, or in a deep state of meditation.

5

TAPPING FOR OUR EMOTIONS

EFT is a powerful tool that can help you understand more about yourself, your strengths, your weakness. It can help you overcome emotional issues and improve relationships.

Before we get started, let me remind you that this book is not intended as a substitute for the medical advice of physicians.

The reader or listener should regularly consult a physician in matters relating to his/her health and particularly with respect to any symptoms that may require diagnosis or medical attention.

In this chapter we'll go into more details and depth on specific issues, including relationships, stress, fears and anxieties, phobias and depression.

RELATIONSHIP ISSUES

One of the basic needs of every human being is to be loved.

When someone feels that he or she is neglected and feels unloved, it naturally creates relationship issues, depression and low self-esteem.

We have a natural tendency to be attracted to others who have similar personality traits.

For example, if you value honesty you are more likely to attract and be attracted to an honest person. If you love yourself you would then you are more likely to meet and attract others towards you.

However, if you hate yourself then you are creating barriers that prevent others from getting close to you and entering your life. Negative feelings like jealousy can seriously harm personal relationships and needs to be addressed.

If you feel that, you are jealous or harbor any negative thoughts either towards yourself or your partner then it's most likely than these thoughts or feelings are also having a negative impact on your relationship. The first step to addressing these issues is to take ownership of them.

Whether you have issues getting close to someone, want to leave a relationship, cope with jealousy, anger or another negative emotion then you can follow the steps below.

TAPPING SCRIPT FOR RELATIONSHIP ISSUES

Below are examples of setup scripts you can use for the tapping procedure. Feel free to modify them so they fit and reflect your own needs.

Even though I am afraid of getting close, I accept my flaws and myself and would be able to overcome these issues.

Even though I had abusive relationships in past, I accept that I can be a better partner and could master courage.

Even though I get jealous, I love and accept myself completely.

Next, tap on your energy meridian points, starting with the karate chop point and then moving down from the head, while reciting your phrase.

Repeat the process and check how well you feel. Do you feel less jealous? Are you more comfortable in the relationship? If you need to, you can repeat the process again.

HOW TO DEAL WITH PERSONAL DIFFERENCES IN A RELATIONSHIP?

When you are in a relationship, there is often a great of personal issues that arise that you will need to take care of, for both you and your partner.

Spending quality time together and speaking openly about personal differences can help you overcome certain obstacles in the relationship.

TAPPING PROCEDURE TO DEAL WITH PERSONAL DIFFERENCES IN A RELATIONSHIP

- Both of you need to sit down together and list down the good qualities you like in your partner.
- Next, write down the qualities you do not like in your partner. I'm aware that this will be difficult, but it's best to be honest.
- Then, write down what all experiences in your relationship made you feel happier (like surprise gifts).
- Now, you need to talk with your partner about what you wrote down emphasizing your good qualities and being honest about the bad.
- *Formulate setup phrases like "Even though I feel lonely when he is at work, I know that he loves me" or "Even though we argue, I know that she loves me". It is a good practice to start with a more insignificant issue.*
- You may end the process by tapping together. You can also

use tapping scripts like *"We love each other and we will work together on our flaws"*.

STRESS

Stress is considered the slow and silent killer. It's effects on the body not only reduce your mood but can compromise your immune system.

Science has shown that stress can reduce life expectancy and it's becoming a bigger problem, affecting more and more people every day.

Today, one of the main causes of stress is work, which can lead to anxiety and depression, in addition to stress.

By effectively utilizing EFT in your day-to-day life, you can fight back at stress.

Here's a few benefits of using EFT and tapping to cope with stress:

- You can feel more motivated and more easily able to achieve your targets
- You can be better able to cope with your anger issues
- You can become more capable of adapting to different situations
- You can be able to work better with your colleagues and clients

Now, let's look at a practical way to put this into action.

TAPPING ROUTINE FOR STRESS

Say these phrases while tapping the karate chop point of your hand:

Even though I feel overwhelmed by the number of things I have to do, I will find peace and clarity.

Even though problems will be created if I don't finish this soon, this unnecessary stress is making me feel overwhelmed, and I want to find peace and quiet.

Even though I have many things to do, I can be more mindful from now on, about what I commit to and what I delegate.

Tap the points of your body shown on the lEFT whilst saying out loud the sentences on the right.

ROUND 1: EXPRESS THE OVERWHELM

Top of the head

I have so many things to do!

Eyebrow

I feel so overwhelmed!

Side of the eye

How am I supposed to get everything done?

Under the eye

I can't believe how much I need to do.

Under the nose

It feels as though I have to climb a massive mountain.

Chin

It seems as though I will never be able to climb to the top

Collar bone

There's so much to do I don't even know where to start.

Under the arm

I will be able to start once I have some clarity.

EFT ROUND 2: UNDERSTANDING THE OVERWHELM

Top of the head

I can think much more clearly when I'm not feeling pressured.

Eyebrow

My head feels it's spinning from the amount of tasks I need to do.

Side of the eye

This is not life or death. Where is the urgency coming from?

Under the eye

Not all of these tasks are urgent.

Under the nose

Some of them need to be done now.

Chin

Some of them can be done later.

Collar bone

Only a few of them are urgent

Under the arm

Worrying about everything at the same time is nonsense

EFT ROUND 3: EXPLORING THE POSSIBILITIES

Top of the head

I'm only creating more pressure on myself

Eyebrow

Wouldn't it be great if everything fell into place?

Side of the eye

Like the pieces of a puzzle?

Under the eye

Without me having to stress out.

Under the nose

Maybe I can prioritize the tasks

Chin

So the most important ones get done.

Collar bone

I will be able to care of those

Under the arm

And feel great for having accomplished something important

EFT ROUND 4: RELAXING

Top of the head

If I just focus on the things of importance

Eyebrow

Then I can reduce the feeling of overwhelm

Side of the eye

Because this feeling is negatively affecting me

Under the eye

And reducing my ability to work

Under the nose

Which is only taking me further away from my goal

Chin

I'm smart enough to prioritize things

Collar bone

I'm going to slow down and focus

Under the arm

And create an effective to do list

EFT ROUND 5: SLOWING DOWN

Top of the head

I just have to slow things down

Eyebrow

There's no to rush through everything

Side of the eye

Things will get done when I'm calm and have clarity

Under the eye

There is great power on being clear about

Under the nose

Knowing what needs to be done

Chin

I'm going to slow down now and focus

Collar bone

This stress is not helping me

Under the arm

I have more control when I'm calm and relaxed

EFT ROUND 6: CHOOSING PEACE AND CALM

Top of the head

I choose to release this stressful energy

Eyebrow

And to focus on doing things that I can do now

Side of the eye

I'm letting go of this feeling of overwhelm

Under the eye

I choose to have a clear mind

Under the nose

I'm going to feel more relaxed and focused

Chin

With every breath I take in and out

Collar bone

I choose to feel good knowing that I'm smart and responsible

Under the arm

I choose to feel calm, confident and powerful

As before, feel free to adapt the wording to suit your own personal circumstances.

FEAR AND ANXIETIES

A certain level of fear and anxiety can be healthy. Fear can safeguard you from dangers while healthy levels of anxiety can help you be organized and ready for anything bad that may happen.

However, when fear is unfounded or irrational and it affects your day-to-day life, then it needs to be remedied. It could potentially undermine your physical and emotional health.

Today, there are a lot of people around the world who suffer from different types of phobias like fear of spiders, fear of war, fear of socializing, fear of heights etc.

Phobia is an excessive or irrational fear of certain objects or situations. People suffering from a phobia usually go out of their way to avoid the stimulus that triggers their fear.

HOW TO HANDLE FEAR AND ANXIETIES WITH THE HELP OF EFT AND TAPPING?

If you are suffering from fear, phobias or anxiety and if the traditional techniques haven't worked for you, then you should definitely try EFT which has helped me people overcome this disorders.

TAPPING TO DEAL WITH FEAR AND ANXIETY

- Rate your anxiety/fear level on scale of 10 (Rate of 10 denotes that issue is most difficult to cope with).
- Identify at what point of time you started to develop this fear. If you are not able to think of the root cause, or when you actually started to develop this fear, you may simply ignore this step. In the latter case, you may frame the tapping script like 'Even though I don't know the cause for the fear, I still accept and love myself'.
- Try to visualize the situation that triggers the anxiety/fear in your mind.
- Use an EFT tapping script based on your situation to help

you overcome the fear or anxiety. *"Even though I have this anxiety a lot of the time, I accept how I feel and still love myself."* Remember you should be tapping your karate chop point whilst you recite this.

- Then tap through the other points on your body starting with the top of the head and working your way down and use a reminder phrase like " *I have this anxiety*".
- Again rate your anxiety level on scale of 10 (Rate of 10 denotes that issue is most difficult to cope with). Evaluate how your anxiety level is compared to before practicing tapping.

You may need to repeat the tapping process couple of times depending on the intensity of the issue.

ANXIETY SCRIPT

After you have finished tapping and reciting your setup phrase like *"Even though I have this anxiety a lot of the time, I accept how I feel and still love myself"* you can use the following script for tapping instead of using the reminder phrase.

For it to be most effective, replace the sentences with your own thoughts and feelings.

Here's a script to start putting the theory into action.

EFT ROUND 1: EXPRESS THE ANXIETY

Top of the head

These anxious feelings that I have

Eyebrow

Are difficult to live with

Side of the eye

There is something I need to do

Under the eye

But this anxiety leaves me feeling paralyzed

Under the nose

It's standing in the way of my success

Chin

It cripples me and leaves me scared

Collar bone

To try new things, go to new places

Under the arm

Or meet new people

EFT ROUND 2: UNDERSTAND THE ANXIETY

Top of the head

I know these feelings

Eyebrow

Are supposed to protect me and prepare me

Side of the eye

But they are just limiting me

Under the eye

They are leaving me afraid

Under the nose

I find it difficult to let go

Chin

The more I think about my anxiety the more it grows

Collar bone

Is something wrong with me?

Under the arm

What can I change?

EFT ROUND 3: EXPLORE THE POSSIBILITIES

Top of the head

Focusing on the anxiety is making it worse

Eyebrow

I keep focusing on what will go wrong

Side of the eye

These thoughts are in my head

Under the eye

And they start with me

Under the nose

If I can shift my focus

Chin

And my attention

Collar bone

To something more positive

Under the arm

I can create more positive thoughts

EFT ROUND 4: RELAXING

Top of the head

I just need to breathe

Eyebrow

And regain my composure

Side of the eye

These thoughts are in my head

Under the eye

Start with me

Under the nose

I will focus on feeling calm

Chin

And relaxed

Collar bone

The slower I breathe in and out

Under the arm

The more relaxed I become

EFT ROUND 5: SLOWING DOWN

Top of the head

I just have to slow things down

Eyebrow

When I am calm and clear

Side of the eye

I will be able to perform better

Under the eye

Because my worries and angst

Under the nose

Will disappear

Chin

I'm going to slow down now and relax

Collar bone

This anxiety is not helping me

Under the arm

I'm much more in control when I'm calm and relaxed

EFT ROUND 6: CHOOSING CALM AND CLARITY

Top of the head

I choose to release this anxious energy

Eyebrow

And to focus on a positive outcome

Side of the eye

When I let go of these fears and doubts

Under the eye

I will be able to succeed to a greater degree

Under the nose

When I'm relaxed and focused

Chin

I can do and achieve anything

Collar bone

I choose to feel good knowing that I'm smart and responsible

Under the arm

I choose to feel calm, confident and powerful

OK, let's move on to a script to help deal with specific phobias.

PHOBIA SCRIPT

After you have finished tapping and reciting your setup phrase like *"Even though I have this fear of needles, I accept how I feel and still love myself"* you can use the following script for tapping instead of using the reminder phrase. Of course for it to be more effective you should replace the sentences with your own thoughts and feelings.

EFT ROUND 1: EXPRESS THE PHOBIA

Top of the head

This phobia that I have

Eyebrow

Is difficult to live with

Side of the eye

It makes me feel embarrassed

Under the eye

It's difficult to talk to people about

Under the nose

It makes going to the doctors a fearful experience

Chin

I worry I will faint

Collar bone

And make a scene

Under the arm

And embarrass myself further

EFT ROUND 2: UNDERSTAND THE PHOBIA

Top of the head

I know this feeling

Eyebrow

Is supposed to protect me and prepare me

Side of the eye

But It's just limiting me

Under the eye

It's leaving me afraid

Under the nose

To receive important medical treatment

Chin

Or donate blood for a good cause

Collar bone

No one else I know has this issue

Under the arm

What can I change?

EFT ROUND 3: EXPLORE THE POSSIBILITIES

Top of the head

Focusing on the negative outcome

Eyebrow

Is just adding power to my fear

Side of the eye

Every time I put off a check up

Under the eye

Because of the fear

Under the nose

I also reinforce that fear even more

Chin

If I can change my focus

Collar bone

To a more positive outcome

Under the arm

Then I can create more positive thoughts and reduce the fear

EFT ROUND 4: RELAXING

Top of the head

I just need to breathe

Eyebrow

And regain my composure

Side of the eye

These thoughts are in my head

Under the eye

Start with me

Under the nose

There is nothing to fear

Chin

Nothing bad is going to happen

Collar bone

I just need to breathe in and out

Under the arm

And allow my mind to become more relaxed

EFT ROUND 5: SLOWING DOWN

Top of the head

I just have to slow things down

Eyebrow

When I am calm and relaxed

Side of the eye

I can focus more on a positive outcome

Under the eye

Which will allow more worries

Under the nose

To disappear

Chin

I'm going to slow down now and relax

Collar bone

This fear is not helping me

Under the arm

It's standing in my way

EFT ROUND 6: CHOOSING CALM AND CONFIDENCE

Top of the head

I choose to release this fearful energy

Eyebrow

And to focus on a positive outcome

Side of the eye

When I let go of these fears and doubts

Under the eye

I will become more confident

Under the nose

When I'm relaxed and confident

Chin

I can do and achieve anything

Collar bone

I choose to feel good knowing that I'm brave and courageous

Under the arm

I choose to feel calm, confident and powerful

Finally, let's look at how EFT might help with depression. Before reading on, please remember that this book is not intended as a substitute for the medical advice of physicians.

DEPRESSION OR DEPRESSIVE THOUGHTS

Today, depression is affecting more and more people, especially in the western world. It can cause us to feel empty, sad and hopeless, which in turn drastically reduces our happiness in life.

Depression is thought to block positive energy and depletes our willpower living us unmotivated to carry out even the simplest of daily activities.

However, using EFT and tapping may help combat depression.

A good example of an EFT setup script that you may use if you suffer from depression would be "Even though I currently suffer from depression, I accept that I will be able to overcome this situation and do well in my life".

DEPRESSION SCRIPT

After you have finished tapping and reciting your setup phrase like *"Even though I feel depressed, I accept how I feel and still love myself"* you can use the following script for tapping instead of using the reminder phrase.

As always, feel free to replace the sentences with your own thoughts and feelings, to make it more personal and effective.

EFT ROUND 1: EXPRESS THE DEPRESSION

Top of the head

This sadness that I have

Eyebrow

Is difficult to live with

Side of the eye

It makes me feel hopeless

Under the eye

It really wears me down

Under the nose

It makes everything seem colourless

Chin

It's sapping my energy

Collar bone

And draining my happiness

Under the arm

It's difficult to open up about it

EFT ROUND 2: UNDERSTAND THE DEPRESSION

Top of the head

What is causing this feeling?

Eyebrow

What is the source?

Side of the eye

Why is it affecting me?

Under the eye

This depression

Under the nose

Is robbing me of my happiness

Chin

And positivity

Collar bone

It's not serving me

Under the arm

How can I fix it?

EFT ROUND 3: EXPLORE THE POSSIBILITIES

Top of the head

I need to see the good in life

Eyebrow

And open myself up to good opportunities

Side of the eye

With both my mind and my heart

Under the eye

Even if things feel difficult to do

Under the nose

They will get easier with time

Chin

If I can change my focus and attitude

Collar bone

To a more positive outcome

Under the arm

Then I can live life more fully

EFT ROUND 4: OPENING UP

Top of the head

I'm willing

Eyebrow

To listen and try new things

Side of the eye

I'm willing

Under the eye

To move on with my life

Under the nose

And leave this sadness behind me

Chin

It serves no purpose

Collar bone

It only drains me

Under the arm

My future can be bright again

EFT ROUND 5: CHOOSING CONFIDENCE AND HOPEFULNESS

Top of the head

I choose to release this negative energy

Eyebrow

And to focus on a positive outcome

Side of the eye

When I let go of this sadness and negativity

Under the eye

I will become more confident and hopeful

Under the nose

When I'm confident and hopeful

Chin

I will become re-energized with life again

Collar bone

This positivity and energy will replace my depression

Under the arm

I will live a good and happy life

NEXT STEPS

OK, so you've read through the scripts and you've probably identified which one you feel is probably the best for you.

In order to experience change and start to see benefits, you need to make a decision.

That is, to start actually tapping.

At first, it may seem strange. But, with persistence, you can start feeling calmer and more in control of your emotions.

To really feel the benefit, you'll want to set aside to tap regularly. By making tapping a habit, it becomes more than a Band-Aid or plaster to use when your emotions get the better or you, or spill over.

If you haven't started yet, when can you set aside 5-10 minutes for your first tapping session?

Once you start to feel the benefits, can you set aside a little time each day to go through the script you feel is most appropriate for that day?

Why not get started today?

7 WAYS TO USE TAPPING TODAY

In our busy, modern day to day lives there are emotional issues common to everybody. With the pressure of personal finance, keeping up with friends and family and being constantly on the go, it's easy to see how people can feel lost and discouraged in modern life.

EFT can give you the power to tap away emotional issues affecting day-to-day mindset and performance.

Let's be honest for a moment. How many times have you felt a little out of control over the last week?

More often than we'd like to say probably.

We all feel the pressure of busy modern life, but if we let our emotions get control of us, situations can quickly get out of control.

Start by using EFT in your day-to-day routine, whenever the emotions start to take over. With tapping, you can help yourself feel safer, more confident and more self aware so you can continue getting on with your day.

Here are seven of the most common day-to-day applications of tapping.

1. ANGER

Anger, frustration, stress, annoyance and all the associated emotions can make up big parts of modern busy life.

Perhaps for you it is a difficult relative, child, boss or co-worker or even road rage that starts you off feeling angry.

Feeling like your space has been breached or offended will bring up negative, angry feelings that can totally change your mood and day.

Here's an example of how EFT changed Andy's life:

Before Andy used EFT, the smallest of slights would set him off. Andy had a closed, self preserving view of the world where everyone could be out to get him at any time!

So whenever someone pushed in line, overtook him on the freeway or spoke bluntly, he was angry that he wasn't being treated fairly. After this anger, it would take hours before he could return to a normal state of mind.

With EFT, Andy was able to tone down his frustrations and cool his anger so he could continue with the day. Before he knew it, what had made Andy angry would slide away like water off a duck's back.

He discovered that there is no better retaliation to anger than overcoming it and getting on with your day!

And learning to overcome anger is something you can do with EFT.

When tapping your sequence, it helps to acknowledge and explicitly state what set you off.

Try this and some of these other phrases to rein in feelings of frustration:

- "I am angry at my {spouse, child, co-worker, etc.}"
- "I am frustrated and angry"
- "This anger will stop me from doing what I need to do"
- "I can't afford this anger"
- "This anger, I can let it go"

2. IMPATIENCE

With the boom in our economies and globalization, it's not a far stretch to have to wait everywhere we want service.

There's queues at the checkout, queues on the phones, queues to get into restrooms, restaurants, queues in traffic – there's simply no escaping waiting.

Impatience is that itching feeling when you need something right away. And oh, boy does it suck when you're engulfed with nothing but impatience.

Here's an example of how EFT changed Sue's life, in her own words:

"I can attest one area of my life I really struggled with impatience was with online shopping.

I'd spend hours and days browsing the online stores, comparing models, and considering exchange rates and shipping prices to find the perfect purchase.

Only after I paid did I realize it would take more than a week to get the item in my hot little hands. More than a week... outrageous!

If the parcel came when I wasn't home, that'd be another day to pick it up from the post office. In the week the parcel would be in transit I'd wait impatiently, fidgety and not in a good mood.

Impatience was controlling me!"

If you find impatience featuring in your life, here's some EFT tapping phrases you can use.

- "I feel impatient, but that's okay"
- "I really want (whatever I want) now, but I can wait"
- "I still have a day to get on with"
- "I won't let impatience stop me from my day"
- "My life will go on while I wait"

3. WORRY

With the convenience of modern life, we all feel as if we're under way more pressure.

All this pressure leads to a very stressful, 21st century life! Things weren't as fast paced as they were a couple of decades ago.

We now need to worry about the looming specter of redundancy, our ability to pay bills and the physical and financial security of ourselves and our loved ones.

When worry plagues the mind, action takes a back seat. Worry hijacks our emotional centres, it rocks the core foundation of our being.

How can you take risks when all you are worried about is the negative outcomes? How can you enjoy life when all that's there is danger? These are the pitfalls of a worrisome life.

Here's what Harry said about his own experience of living with worry:

I know how much worry can control your life. I used to always worry about my financial situation. Several years ago I moved for work, far from family and friends.

Soon after, the company I worked for went through tough times, leaving me worried every day for my job, my livelihood, my rent and my bills.

Worry stopped me from exploring alternate routes to making money.

Only after EFT tapping could Harry overcome his worries, break free from the salary and become the writer and lifestyle coach he is today!

With the emotional freedom technique, you can minimize your worries away to start taking those risks that will help you achieve emotional freedom.

- "I am worried about my situation"
- "I know what I want, but worry is stopping me"
- "I can overcome my worries"
- "I will not let worry stop me from taking action"
- "I am confident and feel secure in myself"

4. LOW SELF-ESTEEM

Low self-esteem is one of the biggest issues people face every day.

Modern life dangles the image of perfection in front of us with every sitcom, movie, reality show, advertisement and magazine.

Physically, magazines demand we have the "perfect abs" or the "firm butt" to get the man or woman we want.

Advertisements sell us lifestyles that we can only dream of, being the envy of family and friends with a big new home, driving along rolling hills in our brand new SUVs, being successful with a new watch or fragrance... the list goes on!

The main message these images sell to you and I, is that we are not good enough as we are right now. Unfortunately, the adverts won't be going away any time soon, but there is one way we can preserve our self-esteem when that nagging feeling emerges – yes, you've guessed it - EFT tapping!

Low self esteem can come from nasty self perceptions within us too. These self perceptions are often borrowed from childhood or some other twisted source. And the truth is, they simply aren't true.

It is shown again and again that we can be most hard on themselves when it comes to self esteem.

However, as a free thinking and self directing adult, you now can start to address your false perceptions of self through EFT.

Try using these phrases whenever low self esteem tries to creep into your life:

- "I don't feel confident in my own skin"
- "I feel like I need to change, but I am perfect as I am now"
- "I am content with my life and myself"
- "I decide what I need in my life"
- "I have the self esteem I need"

5. RESTLESSNESS

Restlessness and lack of sleep is a huge problem in our modern society.

Work has started to follow people home with the mainstreaming of the internet and smart phones. Fizzy energy drinks, caffeine pills, tea, coffee, alarm clocks, fatigue and being on the edge are all symptoms that we, as a culture, have given away precious sleep in exchange for busyness.

So what happens when our head hits the pillow at the end of a busy day?

Well, if you're anything like me back in the day, you'd toss and turn, feel fidgety, be aware of every second that went by and think of what still needed to be done.

Modern life makes it difficult to get to sleep! But with the emotional freedom technique, you may find it easier rest at night. EFT can help you calm down the nervous system and quiet your mind to get proper rest.

When you tap away your restlessness, try these additional techniques:

- Breathe deeply and consciously
- Squeeze your eyelids shut and with your eyeballs, direct them up and inside to the middle of your brow. This activates alpha waves in your brain for deep relaxation
- When you open your eyes, focus them on a point in the distance, either out the window or on your roof

After these additional techniques you can use EFT to tap away your restlessness. Try these mantras or variations for them to get to sleep quickly!

- "I am feeling restless"
- "But my body and mind feels active"
- "This restlessness means I will not get sleep"
- "I need relaxing and restful sleep"
- "I give myself permission to sleep"

6. FEAR OF SUCCESS OR FAILURE

Fear of success and fear of failure are the biggest negative blocks to achieving the life we desire.

Here's something of Paul's story:

For years I was terrified of leaving my job to start my own business. I was too scared of the implications of failing in my business idea.

I'd often ask "What would it mean about me, if my own business failed?" and "What would others think if I failed?"

And on the flip side, the fear of success kept me in a day job: "What would I do with all that money?", "Success isn't for me. After all I only come from a working, middle class background"

Fear gripped me into a state of stasis where I was happy just receiving a consistent monthly pay cheque.

Only until I learnt the controlling grip of fear of failure and success could I step away from my passive, "go with the flow" attitude and direct my life.

If you have a fear of failure or success, you must evaluate your beliefs about failing, money and business.

Look back into your childhood and past to see where these beliefs were formed. If there are any negative emotions there, those are the ones you can target!

Blast those negative feelings away with some EFT phrases:

- "I am afraid of failure/success"
- "I feel I don't deserve success/failure is not acceptable"
- "Failure is not defeat/Success is not evil"

7. PROCRASTINATION

Perhaps the most negative use of time in our modern lives is when procrastination takes over.

I bet you've been there too, 10 minutes of television ends up being 30 minutes and before you know it, your whole night's gone!

Or you wake up in the morning and waste half an hour or an hour just checking your social media, before you even get out of bed.

Technology takes centre stage in our lives. And although technology has increased our productivity and efficiency, our easy access to the internet has made procrastination that much easier, making us less productive!

If we're not careful, a little 'break' at our computers to read the news, watch a movie or check social media ends up wasting a whole hour or maybe far more!

What's worse is when we procrastinate, the time spent often isn't even very enjoyable.

Time spent procrastinating is different to time spent in active mental engagement with hobbies or activities.

How many times have you thought you were winding down or relaxing when in fact, you were just wasting precious time? Ask yourself, do you actually feel better after procrastinating?

I'm guessing that answer is not - it's just something we do, without really thinking about it.

Procrastination doesn't help us take the action needed for the life you love, it isn't entertaining and it doesn't make us feel good.

Whatever reason you procrastinate, there is little to suggest successful, happy people procrastinate all the time.

It is action, not procrastination, that makes the world go around.

It is also action that will help you achieve the emotional freedom you deserve.

Stop procrastination in its tracks with these EFT phrases... right now!

- "I accept I want to procrastinate"

- "I know procrastination is unproductive"

- "I can let go of this feeling to procrastinate"

- "I am in control of my own time"

- "I know what I need to do"

THE SEVEN WAYS

We've looked at seven different ways to use tapping to help manage and control your emotions.

These different emotions included anger, impatience, worry, low self-esteem, restlessness, fear of success or failure and procrastination.

To get the most benefit from this book, go back through and underline or highlight those sections which you feel will be most helpful to you.

That way you'll have them ready, for the next time you start to feel your emotions slipping away from you!

7

CONCLUSION

You've probably heard of the idea of de-cluttering.

De-cluttering is about removing mess and clutter, and bringing order to what was previously disorder.

We all know people who live with clutter in their lives.

Of course, holding onto things isn't necessarily a negative thing. Holding onto items can bring us comfort.

However, when too much stuff weighs us down, instead of bringing comfort, it can cause anger or distress.

Clutter is not only found in physical items but in our emotions.

Emotions build up and, when we fail to deal with them, cause blockages and hindrances in our lives.

By using EFT and tapping, you can experience breakthrough in your emotions.

By continuing to tap regularly, you can feel a shift or change in your mindset. It may even come in a way you didn't expect.

As long as it results in the feeling of being free, a weight being lifted, and being able to make changes for the positive, you'll know you have made progress!

It may take a while for tapping to become a habit, but once it does, you'll be starting to deal with your emotions, before they build up and cause emotional clutter.

Why not make tapping a new habit for you to use, in every area in your life?

By using it consistently, you'll be giving a wonderful gift to give yourself and those around you.

Happy tapping!

AFTERWORD

If you've found this book useful, please consider leaving a rating or review.

You may also appreciate other books by the authors.

CBT for Anxiety : The Psychology of Retraining Your Brain in 21 days

Our thoughts, emotions and behaviours are all connected.

Cognitive Behavioral Therapy offers proven strategies and techniques for anyone suffers with anxiety, panic attacks or compulsive disorders to break free by rewiring your brain.

In this book you'll learn how to:

- identify unhelpful thought patterns and negative thoughts
- retrain your brain to help overcome stress and anxiety
- break bad habits that are holding you back from living the life you want
- become calmer and more confident
- break free and feel 100% happier

Regain control over your life with these proven CBT techniques that you can start using today.

Mindfulness and Meditation for Anxiety - discover proven techniques for helping you deal with your stress and anxiety!

Mindfulness and meditation are not just some hippy idea. They're mainstream, with some of the biggest company names are investing their resources in mindfulness and meditation for their staff.

Studies have shown that mindfulness and meditation can:

- improve the quality and length of sleep
- help focus the mind by reducing distractions
- help you control repetitive thoughts
- improve your memory and mood
- significantly reduce anxiety

By learning how to develop mindfulness and by discovering the power of meditation, you could begin to see the benefits in your life, within weeks.

COGNITIVE BEHAVIORAL THERAPY FOR ANXIETY

THE PSYCHOLOGY OF RETRAINING YOUR BRAIN IN 21 DAYS : OVERCOMING ANXIETY AND COMPULSIVE DISORDERS: PROVEN CBT STRATEGIES FOR LIVING A HAPPIER LIFE

COGNITIVE
BEHAVIORAL THERAPY FOR
ANXIETY

OVERCOMING ANXIETY AND COMPULSIVE DISORDERS:
PROVEN CBT STRATEGIES FOR LIVING A HAPPIER LIFE

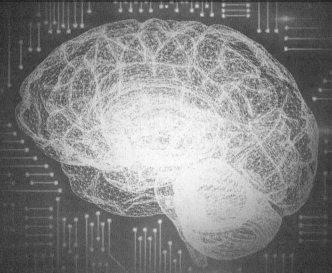

THE PSYCHOLOGY OF RETRAINING YOUR BRAIN IN 21 DAYS

PAUL ROGERS, ROBERT BLOOM

FOREWORD

Welcome to this Cognitive Behavioural Therapy workbook for anxiety.

Cognitive behavioural therapy, or CBT as it's known, is a form of psychotherapy. CBT has been found to be scientifically effective with anxiety and many other mental problems.

We all experience anxiety at some time in our lives, some more than others.

No matter who you are or the underlying cause of your anxiety, this book has been created to help you to deal with any current or recurring episodes of anxiety you may be experiencing.

This book has been written specifically to provide you with the CBT exercises that we, as therapists, use with our clients who are experiencing emotional and mental problems, particularly with anxiety.

We know that CBT works because we've seen it work! And we want it to work for you too. Whatever your problem, we hope that you'll find this book useful and informative.

INTRODUCTION

This book has twenty-one chapters, they're organised into three sections.

The first section is all about you, your experiences and identifying what is actually happening to you.

The second section is all about establishing the CBT techniques which will be most useful to you, and how to employ to get the best results based on your new goals for your life.

The third and final section is all about your new life. You'll learn how to create a strategy for everyday living, that will help you to overcome anxiety, build the support network that will help to keep you well and reduce the chances of new or recurring psychological or emotional disturbances in the future.

This book will provide you with skills, tools and the knowledge and understanding you need to help manage and overcome your anxiety.

In this book we've endeavoured to touch on the most common anxiety disorders that CBT has been proved effective at resolving. If you think that you may need some additional professional input, then don't hesitate to get it!

All the exercises and knowledge in this workbook are indicative of the types of work we do with our clients in one-to-one CBT therapy.

You can use this workbook on your own, alongside a course of CBT treatment with a qualified professional, or with a friend or partner that is supporting you on your journey back to wellness.

Embarking on a course of self-help can be somewhat overwhelming, and we totally understand and appreciate this. Where possible we have made the information and exercises as straight forward and time efficient as possible.

To get the most out of this book, you'll need to commit to the process. Put in as much effort as you can summon, even when you don't feel like you want to.

The good news is that, if you do the exercises, you will see start to see results. Make a point of scheduling some time on a daily basis to work on your anxiety. You'll eventually notice improvements and begin to feel more powerful and self-assured.

Whatever you do, stay with it. Don't worry if you miss a day or two, this doesn't make you a failure. It just makes you human. Sometimes we all lose our way a little.

I'll repeat that - if you miss a day or don't complete an exercise it doesn't make you a failure, it makes you human.

So, with that in mind, we congratulate you on taking this very important first step in dealing with your anxiety. The aim of this book is to help you get well and stay well.

CHAPTER SUMMARY

In Chapter 1, Essentials of CBT, you'll learn more about CBT and why it works. You'll explore what types of anxiety problems CBT has been used to help and learn to identify what your primary issues are.

In Chapter 2, Anxiety and You, we'll explore some of the symptoms of anxiety. We'll look at some commons disorders and problems, associated with anxiety.

We start to look at your ways of thinking and explore the idea of new ways of thinking. You'll start to identify your own behaviours relating to anxiety - anxious behaviours, avoidance behaviours and mood-lowering behaviours.

In Chapter 3, Compulsive Disorders, we look at rituals and compulsions, starting with a quick checklist of compulsive behaviors.

Don't skip this chapter just because you don't think it applies to you! We'll look at Obsessive Compulsive Disorder, also known as OCD. We'll explore Body Dysmorphic Disorder, also known as BDD; and we'll explore Health Anxiety.

We'll begin to delve into managing compulsive disorders, and finish with a practical exercise, to look at your assumptions and how they affect your thinking and behaviours.

In Chapter 4, Is Overcoming Anxiety Possible?, you'll discover how anti-anxiety thinking can help you cope with anxious thoughts.

In Chapter 5, Self-Defeating Strategies, you'll see how your current coping strategies can make your anxiety worse. You'll learn about the importance of confronting situations you fear.

In Chapter 6, Control & Certainty, you'll see how there are limitations to what you can control. People and events are beyond your control. You'll start to look at what your triggers are and how you can make the first steps to living with uncertainty.

In Chapter 7, As a Man Thinketh, you'll learn about the two types of thought that cause anxiety. You'll identify triggers, thoughts and patterns of thinking.

In Chapter 8, Working with Anxious Thoughts, we'll explore some of the most common thinking mistakes human beings tend to make.

We look at common pitfalls and ways of thinking, including all-or-nothing thinking, demand thinking and future telling. We'll get to grips with emotional reasoning, over-generalising, labelling and rating.

You'll get to understand more about mental filtering, disqualifying the positive, low frustration tolerance and personalising. We include some story examples, together with questions, to help you find a positive way to deal with your thoughts.

In Chapter 9, Worry and Anxiety - if worry is also a big part of your life. You'll follow an exercise to help work your way out of the worry maze.

In Chapter 10, Exploring Anxious Emotions, we'll look at healthy and unhealthy emotions. You'll work through an exercise to help you better identify your own emotions.

In Chapter 11, How Our Emotions Work, you'll learn about the four dimensions of human emotions. You'll gain understanding about your action tendencies and begin to see how you can turn unhealthy emotions into healthy emotions.

In Chapter 12, Mindfulness and CBT, you'll find three exercises to help you start practicing mindfulness in your everyday life. You'll learn about how mindfulness and meditation can help you to relax and reduce your anxiety.

In Chapter 13, Can The Future Be Bright Again?, you'll face your fears. Perhaps you believe that the future really can't ever be bright again? This is a chapter of hope - it may take time, but as your brain adjusts, you begin to see that you really can break the habits and patterns of a lifetime.

In Chapter 14, Core Beliefs, you'll see how your past experiences impact your core beliefs about life. You'll start to see how you can identify old unhelpful core beliefs and begin to develop new core beliefs that will positively impact your mental and emotional health.

In Chapter 15, Life Strategy, you'll explore human fallibility. You'll go on an exercise to help you assess your work-life balance and explore how you can improve yours.

In Chapter 16, we'll explore The Problem with Self Esteem, and how developing self-acceptance can be freeing.

In Chapter 17, A New Normal, you'll learn how acceptance can help you feel more comfortable in your own skin.

In Chapter 18, Living Life without Labels, we explore how you can start to replace unhealthy labels with healthy labels.

In Chapter 19, Preventing Relapse into Old Ways, through a series of exercises, we'll look at the practical steps you can take to reduce anxiety.

In Chapter 20, Goal Setting, we'll look at troubleshooting and you'll create your own 'relapse prevention plan' to help you fall back into those old ways.

In Chapter 21, Taking the Theory and Creating A New Reality, you'll learn about two more self-defeating strategies and how to overcome them. You'll explore the issue of self-medication and learn to identify it.

You'll look at how to handle setbacks and how to push forward into your new life, new thinking and new beginning.

Please note that this book is not intended as a substitute for the medical advice of physicians. The reader should regularly consult a physician in matters relating to his or her health and particularly with respect to any symptoms that may require diagnosis or medical attention.

1

THE ESSENTIALS OF CBT

Did you know that the average person has 50,000 to 70,000 thoughts per day? That means that every single minute, you're dealing with between 35 and 48 thoughts.

CBT focuses on the fact that your thoughts, your behaviour and your feelings are all linked. One way of summing up CBT is to say, 'you feel the way you think'.

As the name implies, CBT is a form of psychotherapy that focuses on cognition, that is, your thoughts – and on behaviour, that is, your actions.

The reason CBT also looks closely at behaviour, is because how you think affects how you feel and in turn your feelings affect your actions or behaviours.

If we continue to develop this chain of response further, then the way we act or behave can have a positive or negative influence on our feelings.

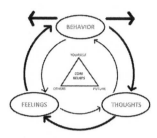

The cycle of thoughts, feelings and behaviour

Without realising it, you may be acting in ways that are actually fuelling negative emotions. In return, this can affect your patterns of thoughts and so the cycle continues. At the core of CBT is this cycle of thoughts, feelings and behaviours.

The development of CBT has come about as a result of scientific testing, evidence-based research and many years of practising the techniques and exercises within the CBT framework to help people with emotional and psychological problems become well.

A big component of CBT involves helping people become their own therapists through the continued use of specific techniques.

This self-directed element is likely one of the reasons people who practice CBT relapse less frequently than those treated using other psychotherapeutic approaches or medications without CBT.

Because of CBT's scientific basis, it invites you to take a more scientific approach to both understanding and resolving your problems.

Throughout this book you will become familiar with a number of terms and phrases, along with techniques that you will pick up as you become efficient in CBT.

Here are some terms it'll be helpful for you to understand:

Cognitive: Everything and anything that occurs in the mind, such as thoughts, dreams, memories, images, repeated patterns of thinking (rumination) and your point of focus.

Behaviour: Everything that you physically and emotionally do, including actions and non-actions. For example, arguing, attacking, avoiding, sulking or brooding.

Therapy: There are many types of therapy. In this case, we are referring to the talking therapies often practised by psychotherapists, that provide solutions for mental, emotional and psychological disturbances.

Belief: Your repeated thoughts create beliefs. Your personal way of viewing the world, other people and situations are all created by your beliefs.

Disturbance: This is an important term that you will come across that refers to any psychological or emotional problem that can cause long-lasting effects to the point of trauma.

Exposure: This term is quite specific to anxiety and refers to the exercise of exposing yourself to the trigger or cause at the root of your anxiety.

This is always done in a managed safe environment and is not to be confused with shock tactics or other negative layman solutions to anxiety.

Trigger: Most thoughts begin as the result of a trigger. This is true whether the thought is new or old.

A trigger can be an actual event, a memory, an image, a past event, a future event, a physical sensation, or your emotions and behaviours.

Triggers aren't limited to actual events that occur in the outside world. They also include internal events such as dreams, heart palpitations, or feelings.

CBT and Anxiety

CBT is an extremely successful treatment in the conditions of depression and anxiety. If you have a doctor or therapist, you may have heard them mention it or you may have heard about it elsewhere.

The techniques and exercises available through CBT work explicitly with the thoughts, emotions and behaviours of a person. These are the key areas in which anxiety is present.

Many people suffering with a form of anxiety will be used to intrusive thoughts and repeated negative patterns of thinking. You may have experienced involuntary or distressing emotions and feelings as a result of these thoughts.

You will experience behaviours, whether conscious or unconscious, that are a direct result of your thoughts, your emotions or both.

Anxiety is an umbrella term that covers a number of disorders and conditions that many people struggle with daily.

You may recognise some of these symptoms:

- a need for control over your mind, health and other personal outcomes
- an intolerance of doubt and uncertainty,
- the desire to take excessive responsibility or ownership of a person or situation,
- obsessive thinking
- rituals or repeated practices
- rumination or stuck thoughts
- anticipating the worst possible outcome
- irrational fears and fearful thinking
- paralysis - the inability to take any action in a situation
- panic and fear of the uncertain

As well as suffering from anxiety, you may also have received one or more of the following diagnoses for an anxiety disorder.

This could include:

- General Anxiety
- OCD
- BDD
- Anticipatory anxiety
- Panic attacks
- Phobia or
- Health anxiety

These are all types of anxiety we will address within this book.

Most importantly, you will be given the understanding, the tools and the skills to manage and overcome these psychological and emotional problems, in order to obtain the freedom to live the live you truly value.

Will CBT work for you?

This is the million-dollar question!

CBT, like any other therapy, depends on your commitment to change.

It will be impacted by your understanding of the therapy and how it will work for you, and of course how much effort you put into the techniques and exercises made available to you here.

Here are a few reasons why CBT can work for you:

1. More and more doctors are recommending CBT because research shows that it helps people to stay well longer.
2. CBT is growing in popularity as an effective treatment for a host of common psychological problems.
3. A lot of research into CBT has focused on its use for the treatment of anxiety in particular, and the results are encouraging.
4. CBT has been proven to be an effective treatment for all of the following problems.

As you read through the list, mentally tick off any that you feel may apply to you.

- Anger problems
- Anorexia
- Binge eating or over-eating
- Body dysmorphic disorder (BDD)
- Bulimia
- Chronic fatigue syndrome
- Chronic pain
- Depression
- Excessive use of alcohol
- Excessive use of prescription and non-prescription drugs
- Feelings of low self-worth
- Gambling and online gambling
- Obsessive-compulsive disorder (OCD)
- Ongoing feelings of guilt or shame
- Panic attacks
- Personality disorders
- Post-traumatic stress disorder (PTSD)
- Social phobia
- Specific phobias
- Spending excessive amounts of money
- Constant worry

You may have checked two or more things on the list here. If so, there's no need to be alarmed. It is very common for problems to overlap.

In fact, one of the many benefits of CBT is that it works extremely well in complex cases. It also helps people to identify additional problems they may have not even acknowledged as contributing to their primary problem.

CBT calls this overlap of two or more problems a meta-emotional problem or a secondary emotional problem.

Luckily the strategies that you use to work on your primary problem usually work on your secondary ones as well.

By implementing CBT techniques, and putting your problems down on paper, you can more easily see how your problems may be interacting with each other.

Writing them down also gives you a clearer starting point for overcoming them.

By listing, and then prioritising your problems, you can begin to identify and unravel how they impact your everyday life and begin to prioritise the targets you want to work on first.

Very rarely will someone suffer from obsessive worry and still get a good night's sleep, for example. Or have panic attacks and social phobia, and be an outgoing, adventurous type.

Example:

Charlie often struggles with going out and as a result has very few friends. He often feels left out of things and dreads going to work.

He has very good relationships, however, with family members and so usually settles for a quiet night in at home in front of the TV.

In this scenario we can see two problems and we can rank them accordingly.

Charlies primary problem is *social phobia - "I don't enjoy going out and so don't push myself to make new friends. This is now impacting on work as well"*.

His secondary problem is feelings of low self-worth. These lead to settling for the comfortable and familiar, but affects Charlies ability to make new friends and relationships.

This is a very simple example, yet you can already see where these symptoms could lead.

If we look at the benefits of targeting these symptoms, in order, we can also see quite clearly the gains and benefits that Charlie could enjoy.

Example:

Anne-Marie struggles with a fear of what could happen. She is required to travel and meet with clients for her job and dreads it every time she has to make a trip.

As a result, she will avoid booking tickets for her journeys and will even reschedule meetings or pass them on to others, in order to avoid the negatively anticipated outcome.

She often lets clients down or misses out on promotions, increased responsibilities and new opportunities.

In this scenario we see a number of different problems than the ones Charlie is struggling with. So, let's look at how we can rank these in a similar way.

Anne-Marie's primary problem is *anticipatory anxiety.* "*I'm afraid if I do this, then something terrible might happen, so I avoid or delay the activity*".

This is now creating greater anxiety in her job, making her afraid she could lose it or that she will never progress.

Her secondary problem is constant worry about her job, which leads to settling for 'safer' or easier roles or tasks, but affects her ability to progress in her career.

Identifying Any Problems

The examples above show how you may have multiple problems and how they can be ranked.

Consider the items on the list above that you checked.

Rank them in order of importance of the most deep-seated or severe problem, that is affecting your quality of life.

While you may struggle to identify which is the most severe, the list above will help you to at least identify your problems and then you can decide which is impacting your life negatively the most.

Exercise:

Once you have selected your problems, try ranking them and then putting them into real life examples so you can see quite clearly how they are affecting your life.

Once you have completed this exercise move onto the next chapter.

2

ANXIETY AND YOU

At its most basic, anxiety is what you feel in response to a real or perceived threatening situation.

You may experience anxiety in different ways:

- As extreme fear in the case of phobias
- overwhelming physical feelings in the case of panic disorder, or
- as a relatively constant feeling of unease and agitation

Anxiety comes in many different forms and it can affect just about anyone, from any walk of life.

Anxiety is not fun at all. It can be extremely unpleasant and uncomfortable. It's completely understandable that you may wish to stop your symptoms and learn to control them.

Unfortunately, these attempts to fight against the physical feelings of anxiety almost always have a paradoxical effect.

You actually end up panicking about your anxious feelings and, by trying to eliminate or control them, you actually worsen and perpetuate them.

Your attempts to avoid, stop, or reduce physical sensations are also known as *safety behaviours*.

Here are some anxiety symptoms you may have experienced:

- Difficulty concentrating
- Feeling dizzy or lightheaded
- Dry mouth
- Surroundings seem distant or unreal
- Neck tension
- Thoughts racing
- Difficulty swallowing
- Shoulder tension
- Wobbliness in legs
- Tingling in extremities
- Heart pounding or racing
- Cold sweats
- Sweaty palms
- Feeling hot
- Feeling unsteady
- Trembling hands
- Tightness in chest
- Frequent urination
- Butterflies in stomach
- Nausea

If you have real health concerns worthy of medical investigation, see your doctor. Getting a clean bill of health from your physician, prior to launching yourself into CBT exercises, may help you to normalise your uncomfortable physical symptoms of anxiety.

If you suffer from health anxiety, however (and worry that you may have a serious disease or illness despite evidence to the contrary), resisting seeing the doctor for frequent reassurance that you're not in ill health is probably in your best interest.

Severe anxiety can really interfere with your ability to live a satisfying life. At its worst, you may find that your anxiety restricts your socialising, prevents you from doing your job, or stops you from leaving your house.

Some people become anxious following a specific, identifiable traumatic event. More often, however, anxiety slowly builds up, without you being able to put your finger on a definite cause.

We're going to start by looking at how to confront anxiety and overcome it. No matter what form your anxiety takes, the techniques in this chapter are likely to be useful to you.

It can be helpful to have a clear diagnosis of your particular type of anxiety problem. However, you can use this book to overcome your anxiety whether you've been given a formal diagnosis or not.

Your doctor or psychiatrist may have diagnosed you with an anxiety disorder or you may recognise symptoms within yourself.

Whatever the case, you will find within these pages the skills and techniques you need to overcome your anxiety.

Let's look at some common anxiety disorders. Don't be put off by the long-sounding names, these are just medical terms to describe differing types of anxiety.

Common anxiety disorders include:

- *Generalised anxiety disorder* (GAD) feeling anxious to varying degrees almost all of the time.
- *Obsessive-compulsive disorder* (OCD) which is characterised by unwelcome intrusive thoughts and a compulsion to carry out elaborate rituals in an unrealistic effort to prevent feared events from happening.
- *Panic attacks* - these often lead people to believe that they're

having a heart attack, about to pass out, or even die because the physical sensations are so strong. Panic attacks may occur in specific situations or they can just seem to come out of the blue.

- *Phobias* - as we all know are specific fears of everyday things or situations. These are sometime referred to as irrational fears because the degree of fear experienced is out of proportion to the actual threat involved.
- *Post-traumatic stress disorder* (PTSD) is a state of anxiety resulting from a traumatic event which was life threatening or significantly threatened a person's physical integrity. People can develop PTSD from witnessing an event that lead them to feel extreme fear and horror.

You will more than likely be familiar with these ways of thinking:

- Overestimating the probability of a threat or a bad ending to an event or situation
- Overestimating how bad it would be if the threat or bad ending actually happened
- Underestimating your ability to cope with the threat or bad ending

As you follow the exercises in this book and apply them, you'll learn to

- be realistic about the probability of any threat
- put the severity of the threat or negative situation into perspective
- give yourself some credit for your coping abilities

You'll learn new ways of thinking, such as:

- 'It could happen but it's not as likely as I imagine'.
- 'It's bad but not terrible, unfortunate but not awful, difficult but not disastrous, hard but not horrid'.
- 'It's uncomfortable but I can stand it',
- 'it's difficult to cope with but I can cope'
- 'it's hard to bear but it's still bearable'

Anxious Behaviours

Living with anxiety in and of itself is not the only challenge you will be facing. As a result of anxiety, you may be exhibiting some negative or bad behaviours.

CBT understands that disturbed emotions tend to lead to destructive and self-destructive behaviours.

You may or may not have the intention of dealing with the poor behaviours. Destructive behaviour rarely aids effective problem solving. In fact, destructive and self-destructive behaviour often creates further problems or makes existing ones worse.

Use the following checklist to help you to identify different types of bad, and self-destructive behaviours that you may sometimes recognise yourself doing.

Be honest with yourself as you go through the three lists below.

Take time to review these three lists of avoidance, mood lowering and self-destructive behaviours and identify which behaviours you notice in yourself.

Avoidance Behaviours

- Avoiding exercise
- Doing other unrelated tasks rather than doing what actually needs to be done (such as tidying your desk rather than writing an essay)

- Engaging in superstitious behaviour in an attempt to ward off feared events
- Not answering the phone
- Not opening post (such as bills)
- Not speaking much in social gatherings
- Putting off tasks
- Staying away from situations that you find threatening (lifts, busy places, parties, and so on)
- Using rituals to help quell anxious thoughts and feelings

Mood lowering Behaviours

- Isolating yourself from friends and family
- Letting daily chores mount up
- Neglecting your hygiene
- Not asking others for help or support
- Not engaging in activities, you usually enjoy
- Repeatedly calling in sick at work
- Sleeping too much or too little
- Staying in bed all day
- Staying indoors most of the time
- Stopping taking your medication

Self-destructive behaviours

- Drinking excessively
- Eating poorly (too much or too little)
- Engaging in high-risk sexual activities
- Gambling
- Lashing out verbally or physically
- Spending money compulsively or recklessly
- Sulking
- Taking risks when angry (such as reckless driving)
- Using illegal drugs

The more items you've ticked off on the checklist, the more probable it is that you're experiencing emotional disturbance. In turn, your 'bad' behaviours are almost certainly making things worse for you and those around you.

If you're sick and tired of living with anxiety and you want to return or gain the freedom that you believe can be available to you, keep reading.

In writing this book, we do not wish to minimise or dismiss any of your thoughts, feelings or real experiences caused by anxiety. As you begin this journey, try your very best to adopt an attitude of can, shall and will, rather than can't, won't, shouldn't or shall not.

Anxiety lives in the shadows of your mind and thrives in the darkest recesses of your lives.

Anxiety wants you to believe that it is much bigger, more powerful and stronger than you and the simple truth is that it isn't.

You can learn techniques to help you master it. No matter how long you have been suffering, no matter the extent of your anxiety.

It's time for a new beginning. The start of a new attitude, a new belief, a new way of life and a new normal.

3

COMPULSIVE DISORDERS

When we begin to explore anxiety a little deeper we come across compulsive disorders, these are some of the most well-known forms of anxiety and present as intrusive thoughts and repeated unrealistic rituals.

Don't be tempted to skip this chapter. You may feel uncomfortable about the idea of 'compulsive disorders', but meeting these head on and without fear, is the start of moving on to your new life.

So, what are compulsions? These are actions that you feel compelled to carry out over and over again usually in a precise and exact manner. Health anxiety, OCD, and BDD all involve compulsive actions and rituals.

Rituals and compulsions are largely similar. For both, you feel the need to complete them and feel very uncomfortable and anxious if you're somehow prevented from doing so.

Rituals are often more elaborate than straightforward compulsions. A typical example would be the hand washing for a number of times before feeling that your hands are clean or checking the house numerous times before feeling that it is safe enough to leave it.

These may not sound too serious, that is, until hand washing leads to infections and sores on the hands as a result of washing too many times with products that are damaging to the skin. Or when checking the house so many times it leads to being late for everything and eventually never or rarely leaving the house because of the incessant fear of leaving it unsecured.

Example:

Sally loved to shop online. She would enjoy picking out bargains and new fashions when she got paid at the end of the month. Sally's excitement at the pending deliveries would be palpable. Often times however the clothes that arrived would be a little on the tight side or maybe even a little big, due to the manufacturing and this would send Sally into a tailspin of doubt about her size, shape and body image.

Sally would repeatedly ask friends and family if she has gained weight or looked older. She would be relentless for hours, seeking words of reassurance, while still doubting everything she was being told. This could last for days and take many weeks before Sally would pluck up the courage to get back online and pick out new outfit choices.

The following exercise will help you to identify any compulsions or rituals you may be living with, in order to address them, expose them and begin the recovery process from them.

Exercise:

We're going to look at a compulsions checklist now. How many of the following apply to you?

- I frequently check things such as locks, water taps, gas taps, electrical items more often than is necessary.

- I spend an excessive amount of time washing.
- I frequently seek reassurance from my partner, friends, or family.
- I frequently repeat words and phrases in my mind, or replay images.
- I spend an excessive amount of time putting things in order, tidying, or making things 'just so'.
- I have an excessive amount of clutter and hoarded items in my home.
- I try hard to push upsetting thoughts out of my mind.
- I become significantly distressed if I'm prevented from or am interrupted in carrying out my rituals.
- My compulsions interfere with my ability to function in important areas of my social life, work, family life, and relationships.

How many of these statements did you agree with? All of these are compulsions of some kind.

As you become aware of any compulsions or rituals that are present in your life, you have a clearer idea of what you need to be doing less of.

Not sure if these apply to you, or how much? You may find it helpful to have a compulsion diary, so you can monitor how many times you check things, repeat words or phrases, ask for reassurance, or engage in other rituals.

You may also want to record exactly how much time you spend on certain tasks. Doing this can help you fully realise the degree to which compulsions are interfering with your life.

Once you have identified the frequency you can begin the process of reducing the number of times you engage in each compulsion or ritual and keep a daily record to show your progress.

If you happen to fall off and return to the original number at any point, do not stop. Simply remind yourself that you are human and begin the process again. Take it very gradually and reduce the numbers incrementally. Bear in mind that reducing and stopping these actions is a major element in overcoming your compulsions.

Obsessive Compulsive Disorder (OCD)

OCD is a broad topic. There are many different forms of OCD and while we will not be able to discuss all of the forms within this book [OCD needs its own encyclopaedia] the good news is, that however severe your OCD, CBT can help you to overcome it.

OCD is in the top ten most disabling illnesses, according to the World Health Organisation. This illness is characterised by obsessions, which are distressing thoughts, images, impulses, or doubts, and compulsions, which are rituals and regimented behaviours that a person feels compelled to perform.

CBT has proven to be successful in helping people overcome each of the obsessional problems that we discuss in this book.

OCD is what called a spectrum disorder, which means that it can range in severity. People with mild OCD may find their obsessions irksome but are not bothered by them for more than an hour each day and their OCD doesn't stop them from living a normal life. If you have more severe OCD, you probably find your obsessions very distressing and distracting.

Your obsessions are on your mind for at least an hour and possibly several hours every day. While only a doctor can diagnose OCD, you will be able to identify whether you have a mild or sever form of OCD by completing the following checklist.

Example:

Mike was a fitness guy and loved to work out in his local gym. He often trained for 2 or more hours a day and would always look forward to returning home after a good workout. He looked forward to resting and having a nice meal, but a part of him also wanted to make sure the house was safe and secure, because he had experienced a break in a few years earlier.

Prior to the break in, Mike would check the windows and locks on the doors to make sure the house was safe.

Nowadays he would check every window and door thoroughly before leaving, starting with the windows at the top of the house.

He'd open and close each bedroom window to make sure it was locked, and then progress to the downstairs windows.

Then he would return back upstairs to check that he had closed all of the doors, to delay any intruders, and then make sure that the front and back doors were all securely bolted before leaving.

Exercise:

Let's have a look at another compulsions checklist. How many of the following apply to you?

- Distressing unwanted religious, blasphemous, sacrilegious thoughts or images intrude into my mind.
- I am greatly troubled by intrusive thoughts or images of violent acts such as stabbing, pushing, hitting, burning.
- Unacceptable or inappropriate sexual thoughts or images repeatedly enter my mind against my will and cause me distress.
- I frequently worry about contamination from dirt, germs, bodily fluids, excrement, chemicals, sticky substances, or other material.
- I frequently worry greatly that I might lose something important or regret throwing something away.
- I often worry that I might be responsible for a bad event such

as a fire, flood, car accident, or burglary through not being careful enough.

These are very common types of OCD. Ticking even one is sufficient to indicate that you're suffering with OCD.

It's not uncommon for individuals to have more than one form of obsession, so don't be alarmed if you tick more that one of the first six items.

Now, *please answer yes or no to each of the following statements*:

- My obsessions cause me significant levels of distress.
- My obsessions are on my mind for at least an hour each day.
- My obsessions interfere with my ability to function in important areas of my life such as my social life, work, family life, and relationships.

These last three questions can help you determine how severe your problem is and how much it's disrupting your life.

As we show, understanding what your problem is a critical step in ridding yourself of excessive and disabling anxiety, obsessions, and preoccupations.

The way you currently choose to cope with your obsessions may be part of maintaining them – in other words, your solution may be the problem. Understanding this is a really important part of recovering.

Body Dysmorphic Disorder (BDD)

The American Psychiatric Association says body dysmorphic disorder is characterised by a preoccupation with an imagined defect in appearance or markedly excessive attention to a minor physical defect.

BDD is a profoundly distressing and disabling problem that goes far beyond imagined ugliness.

Sufferers tend to be very preoccupied with their appearance and highly afraid of being humiliated because of what they perceive as their 'revolting' or 'freakish' looks.

Exercise:

Complete the checklist below, to discover whether you may be suffering from BDD.

- I spend more than an hour each day worrying about my appearance.
- I believe that I look ugly or unacceptable, despite being reassured by others that this is not the case.
- I worry that I will be embarrassed or humiliated because of my appearance, especially if I don't conceal or camouflage my defect(s).
- I tend to compare my appearance to that of other people, including people I encounter in my real life and those in magazines and on television.
- I spend a lot of time thinking about how I might improve or camouflage my appearance through cosmetic or dermatological procedures, clothing, dietary supplements, exercise, make-up, and so on.

How many of these did you agree with? If you agreed with three or more of items, you're probably suffering with BDD.

The same CBT techniques that work for OCD can help you overcome BDD. The exercise at the end of this chapter to help you understand and overcome BDD.

Health Anxiety

Hypochondriasis is the old term for health anxiety, which has now been dropped by professionals as it suggests someone who is constantly suffering from different ailments and is a bit neurotic.

In fact, real health anxiety can be severely distressing. It involves being preoccupied with constant worries about having or developing serious illnesses. The checklist below will help you to identify whether this is a condition you are suffering from.

Exercise:

Here's a checklist, to help you discover whether you may be suffering from health anxiety. How many of the following apply to you?

- I spend at least an hour a day worried by a fear of being ill or an idea that I am ill with cancer, heart disease, multiple sclerosis, AIDS, or something similar despite having been given medical reassurance.
- I have a strong sense that I am vulnerable to illness.
- I worry that if I'm not vigilant for signs of illness I might miss something important.
- I worry a lot that anxiety itself may cause harm.

If you agreed with the first item (that is, you spend at least an hour a day worried by a fear of being ill or an idea that you are ill), that alone probably indicates that you have health anxiety.

If you agreed with the first item and one or more other items, the probability that you suffer from health anxiety increases.

Obsessive-compulsive disorder, body dysmorphic disorder, and health anxiety all respond very well to CBT treatment.

The same CBT exercises are effective in overcoming all three of these disorders, which is why they have all been included in this chapter on Compulsive disorders.

The exercise at the end of this chapter will help you to overcome Health Anxiety also.

Managing Compulsive Disorders

When working with Compulsive disorders and CBT 'How can you know for sure?' is the question that comes up most often.

- How can you be sure I won't cause someone harm?
- How can you be sure I'm not ill?
- How can you be sure I won't get ill?
- How can you know I won't be rejected and humiliated?
- How can you be sure I'm not dangerous to children?

The answer, of course, is that we can't be sure of any of these things. But we can be pretty sure that if you keep searching for answers to these doubts and uncertainties you're likely to maintain your obsessional problem.

If you identified an obsessional problem in yourself and are worried about something, you can't be certain that your fear won't come true. However, you can be fairly sure that you're likely to over-estimate the chances of disaster.

This knowledge has a very important implication. Instead of worrying, you can choose to safely assume that things are okay and then act accordingly.

Example:

Janet worked as a nurse and was very good at her job. She was often called upon by others due to her experience and knowledge and took her role very seriously. Patients felt very safe with her, and Janet related to them very easily.

This wasn't the case a few years ago, when a patient died while in Janet's care. As a result of this happening she began to have anxious thoughts about what she could or should have done differently and how she could have affected a different outcome for the patient and the patient's family. She began to believe that she wasn't a good nurse and would harm other patients and began to seriously consider a new career.

Thankfully Janet was referred to a counsellor at work where she began to acknowledge her fears and develop the tools to move past the obsessive thoughts of being dangerous to patients.

Now whenever Janet notices these obsessive thoughts, she tells herself that patients dying is an occupational hazard and that she is more likely to help somebody get better than have them die in her care.

Although she still has anxious and obsessive thoughts, Janet now has a more balanced approach and while she can't be sure that a patient will not die in her care, it is not a definite outcome for every patient in her care.

Exercise:

Think of your mind as a leaf on the river, travelling along in normal weather conditions. As your mind floats along, the left-hand side of the river becomes the negative assumptions you automatically make, and the right-hand side becomes the alternative assumptions you will guide yourself towards.

You are the current that decides which way the leaf goes and whether the leaf will be caught on the bank or make it all the way along the stream.

Write full answers to the statements below.

Negative Assumptions:

What I tend to assume:

How I act as a consequence:

The results of thinking and acting in this way:

Alternative (assuming things are okay) assumption:

What I tend to assume:

How I act as a consequence:

The results of thinking and acting in this way:

. . .

Here is an example of what this could look like:

Jack is a middle-aged man who often struggles with his general health. He is a smoker, enjoys a beer with friends several times a week, and despite his girlfriend's best efforts for him to eat well, he enjoys the occasional Kebab. He doesn't like to visit the doctor and prefers to look up symptoms on the internet when he is feeling particularly ill.

Take a look at Jack's answers following the exercise:

Negative Assumptions:

What I tend to assume: That I'm going to die early because I'm so unhealthy

How I act as a consequence: I carry on because I know that if I don't have cancer already, I'll probably get it soon

The results of thinking and acting in this way: I don't try and eat healthy, I won't quit smoking and I still drink very often.

Alternative (assuming things are okay) assumption:

What I tend to assume: Even though I don't always feel well, I'm not seriously ill, and I should get a proper medical opinion on my health

How I act as a consequence: I book an appointment for a check-up with my doctor. I cut back on drinking and smoking and try to eat better

The results of thinking and acting in this way: I get an actual medical diagnosis for my health, I find out if there is help for me to stop smoking and cut back on drinking, and I take steps towards living a healthier life, so I don't have to always worry about my health.

Going Forward

People with obsessional problems like OCD, BDD, and health anxiety typically demand cast-iron guarantees that certain bad things won't happen. This is unrealistic and very rarely will be met.

When doing this exercise, use it sparingly to help you observe and manage your control triggers, and avoid this becoming yet another ritual.

Use it to practice noticing and actioning alternative assumptions to your current natural way of thinking. When you're working to overcome obsessional problems, it's important to learn to tolerate doubt and uncertainty.

4

IS OVERCOMING ANXIETY POSSIBLE?

Anxiety frequently leads you to make a feared event more terrible in your own mind than it actually is in real life.

When you're riddled with anxiety you tend to inflate bad or negative events out of proportion, deciding that they're awful, world ending, and unbearable.

Thankfully, events are rarely this bad. Most of the time you'd cope with your feared event, no matter how uncomfortable and difficult it may be.

Overcoming anxiety is possible with the help of CBT.

CBT techniques include a way of thinking which we refer to as anti-anxiety thought process or thinking. Using this technique, you develop a new way of thinking, of processing events and situations. You may not initially believe these new thoughts.

With practice, CBT can help reduce any anxiety you may be experiencing.

Your first step in Anti-anxiety thinking is to increase your belief in:

- Your ability to cope with distressing or uncomfortable situations
- Your ability to manage unpleasant feelings and emotions
- Your ability to pull yourself out of unhealthy thought patterns
- Your ability to prevent or minimise unhealthy behaviours

When you do this, you can remind yourself of the following:

- You have coped with situations just or bad or worse before
- You have come through episodes of intense fear or panic before
- You have managed difficult thoughts or emotions without rituals or compulsions before
- You have come through intensely uncomfortable experiences before.

Your next step is to develop a healthier attitude to the way people think of you or view you.

This includes understanding that:

- You can't please all of the people all of the time
- It's not necessary to change your opinion of yourself according to others opinion of you
- It's unfortunate if others think badly of you, but it's not the end of your world
- It isn't nice if you embarrass or humiliate yourself publicly, but it isn't unbearable

It's important to practice being more compassionate and forgiving towards yourself. Allow 'bad' things to happen sometimes, and remember to congratulate yourself when you get through them.

5

SELF-DEFEATING STRATEGIES

The last thing you want to do when you feel anxious or your anxieties are in full effect is to face your anxiety head on.

When you're having a full-blown panic attack as a result of your agoraphobia, it can feel almost impossible to leave the house.

When your Health Anxiety has convinced you're dying from cancer, it might feel impossible to visit the doctors. You don't want to hear the actual diagnosis.

CBT teaches that the more you confront the situations you fear, the more likely you are to extinguish your fear. You'll also increase your conviction in your ability to negotiate such situations successfully.

Once you begin to implement the strategies and techniques given to you in this book, you can begin to move away from any safety behaviours or self-defeating strategies you have in play.

You can begin to strengthen your resolve and belief that you can and will achieve the next level of your recovery.

You probably aren't aware of perpetuating your problems with some of your coping behaviors. Some people don't know exactly how to best help themselves overcome problems such as anxiety.

As an anxiety sufferer, you'll have safety behaviours. These can include hiding, rituals, justification through thoughts, sulking or anger.

When you feel threatened as a result of your anxiety you may decide to avoid the very thing that you fear. When a friend encourages you to take a walk to the store, you may decide to express anger.

Perhaps you dive into a ritual to overcome the nagging thoughts and emotions that present themselves when you think of a past event or trauma.

Identifying Self-Defeating Strategies

A self-defeating strategy is one that's meant to solve a problem but actually causes more problems than it solves, because it causes the same or other problems.

The first step in identifying your self-defeating strategies, is recognising which of your tactics are actually maintaining your problems, or making them worse.

Here are some examples of what we mean by self-defeating strategies or safety behaviours:

Avoiding situations that you fear or that provoke anxiety.

Taking drugs or using alcohol to block out uncomfortable emotions.

Hiding aspects of yourself that you feel ashamed about.

Putting off dealing with practical problems and tasks that you find unpleasant.

Withdrawing from your usual routine.

Isolating yourself from friends and family.

Worrying - many people think that by worrying about potential negative events they will prevent bad things from happening or prepare themselves to deal with such events. Although worrying may seem like a way of solving or preventing future problems, it actually becomes a problem itself because it promotes anxiety.

Performing rituals - people who suffer with anxiety disorders like obsessive-compulsive disorder often insist that they perform everyday tasks like dressing or cleaning themselves in a very rigid, ordered pattern. They often worry that if they fail to execute tasks in a precise way that something bad will happen to themselves or others as a result. If the pattern is interrupted, these people become very anxious and often make themselves begin the ritual all over again, and may spend hours trying to get their rituals done exactly right.

Checking things over and over - it's normal to check that you've locked the door or that you've got your keys in your bag once or twice. But people with anxiety problems often check things like this so many times that they find it very difficult to leave the house and arrive at work or appointments on time.

You may be using many more possible troublesome tactics in addition to the ones listed here. The type of coping strategies you choose will depend on the type of problems you're experiencing.

In CBT we encourage you to drop your troublesome coping tactics in favour of healthier behaviours. These healthier behaviours can ultimately help you overcome your problems.

This approach can mean doing things that cause you short-term anxiety or discomfort in the spirit of getting well.

When you first recognise and then drop your 'safety behaviours' you can feel worse in the short term. However, by learning healthier behaviours, you will benefit in the long run. You may feel worse, before you feel better.

Leaving the safety behaviours behind will allow you to see that you can withstand the feelings of anxiety, or general discomfort and self-consciousness you may feel, by doing nothing at all to stop them.

The bottom line is that although anxiety, embarrassment, social awkwardness, and self-consciousness are unpleasant, none of these things are going to kill you.

6

CONTROL AND CERTAINTY

If you suffer from an anxiety problem such as post-traumatic stress, obsessive compulsive disorder, or panic attacks, you probably want to be in control.

In fact, you probably demand control in all situations and insist on certainty as much as possible.

The trouble is that you're trying hard to control things that are *beyond* your control. For example, other people's thoughts and behaviours, or even your own thoughts.

No matter how hard you try, many things exist in life that you simply can't be 100 per cent certain about.

If you continue to try to be in a state of absolute control and utter certainty at all times, you're likely to become even more anxious.

If you can learn to accept limitations to your personal power and live with uncertainty, it can really make a positive difference to how you feel.

It's important for you to give other people permission to make their own decisions and form their own opinions, even though it means losing an element of control.

Example:

Shirley and Peter have been married for 15 years and are currently in relationship counselling. They are finding it very difficult to agree on much in their relationship.

Although there has been no infidelity in the marriage, every time he leaves the house without her, Shirley is convinced that Peter is on the verge of cheating on her.

This has led to Peter becoming distant from his wife, because he knows she doesn't trust him. This, in turn, has led Shirley to mistrust Peter even more.

During counselling Shirley learned that the infidelity she saw in her older sisters marriage, her best friends relationship and the main character in her favourite soap had led to a belief that all men will cheat at some point.

Shirley had begun to try and control Peter's behaviour, so she could be certain that she wouldn't suffer the same fate as her sister and best friend.

Although the therapists encouragement of Peter being more communicative began to ease some of the strain in the marriage; it was primarily Shirley's new behaviour that had the greatest impact.

Shirley began to understand that her core belief of all men being unfaithful was not founded in truth. She realised that she couldn't control Peter mentally, emotionally or physically. So, she began the process of releasing the need for control and certainty in her marriage.

Although the couple are still in therapy, their marriage is in a healthier place. They are both learning new skills and tools that help Shirley to accept the limitations of her personal power.

Shirley is learning to accept that, even if Peter was unfaithful, she would live. Therefore she was able to finally give him the permission to be an adult and manage his own behaviour.

Trying to control how others behave and what they think about you is common.

However, it's a fruitless endeavour, because other people are outside your sphere of control.

You can't control what other people do or think most of the time. You may be able to influence or request others to behave and think in desired ways, but it's ultimately up to them to decide on their own thoughts and actions.

The same goes for life events you experience. Life is often unpredictable, uncertain, and even downright unfair. By insisting that you need certainty about what life is about to deal you, at all times, you're likely to experience a lot of anxiety.

No-one can control random life events and trying too hard to do so will only generate further worry, stress and anxiety.

Try writing down what your own control triggers are here.

....

....

....

....

Now write down an accompanying statement as to what you can do differently.

....

....

Complete the following sentences for each trigger you identify.

Trigger:

....

....

....

What I tend to assume:

....

....

How I act as a consequence:

....

....

The results of thinking and acting in this way:

....

....

Alternative (assuming things are okay) assumption:

....

....

How I can act as if I'm assuming things are okay?

....

....

The Uncertainty of Life

If something negative happened to you once, you're more likely to assume that you're vulnerable to the same sort of bad event happening to you again.

This is rarely true. However, you may go to great lengths to try to get a guarantee that nothing bad happens in your life.

After a traumatic event, it's understandable that you might feel this way. However, it's not a helpful way to look at the world.

Living with uncertainty is part of being human. It's something we all do every day, although you may not realise it. Work on accepting the idea that life is uncertain and always has been.

Your attempts to be totally in control and certain are contributing to your anxiety, not reducing it. Your need to control and be certain about things, will often lead to disappointment. When your needs are not met, it can produce more anxiety-inducing thoughts and emotions.

Example:

Obsessive fortune-telling that your partner will cheat when they are not with you, demonstrates a need for control and a fear of losing control of this person.

We cannot control others, only ourselves. We each have our own thoughts, feelings and intentions.

It's time to face up to and move past the thoughts and feelings that make you feel uncomfortable. You cannot control other's actions.

You may have fearful thoughts of others doing things you will not like or approve of. You may catastrophise. You may constantly look to others for reassurance and certainty that everything is going to be alright.

It's important to acknowledge that, in life, nothing is 100% certain.

There are so many things in life that are outside of our control. Life happens.

We must release as much as possible our need to be in control and feel certain, accepting that there are limitations to our personal power and ability.

7

AS A MAN THINKETH

CBT has a strong focus on thoughts and patterns of thinking. This is the cognitive part of Cognitive Behavioural Therapy.

The key objective in this chapter is to give you the tools to begin thinking in a balanced and healthy way.

When this starts to happen in your life, you should notice a significant reduction in your anxiety and better regulation of your emotions.

The following statement is at the core of CBT and why it works.

The way you think about specific events in your life, and the meaning you give to these events, determines how you feel and act in response to them.

It makes good sense to learn how to 'catch' these thoughts.

You have two ways to deal with these thoughts. You can either turn them from negative to positive, or allow them to pass without acting on them.

Each of us has two types of thoughts that can cause anxiety. These are automatic thoughts and rumination.

Automatic thoughts are the ones that seem to just pop into your head without warning, hence automatic.

Frequently, our automatic thoughts can be distorted. Automatic thoughts can be unhelpful ways of interpreting an event or situation.

Most of us don't notice these automatic ways of thinking. If you're aware of these automatic thoughts, you may not question how true or useful they are.

Rumination is the process of chewing on a thought, repeating the same thought over and over.

Rumination is usually present in compulsive disorders and phobias. The same recurring thought becomes reality for the thinker. They go over and over the same thoughts, images or ideas.

Most of our thoughts begin as the result of a trigger.

Triggers can be an event, a memory, an image, a past event, a future event, a physical sensation, or your emotions and behaviours. Triggers can include internal events such as dreams, heart palpitations, or our feelings.

When we learn to recognise our thoughts, we can begin the process of understanding them and determining whether they are useful to us or not.

We can determine whether our thoughts are healthy or unhealthy or, in simple terms, positive or negative.

Example:

Maria was a worrier. She would often ruminate on her problems, other people's problems and even the world around her. Maria was ruminating so much that she would often lose focus on her work, lose concentration when reading a book or even miss the end of a movie, all because she would get carried away with her thoughts.

One day while driving Maria lost complete concentration and was jolted back to the present moment when she hit the car in front of her. Although everyone was ok, and there was very little damage, Maria made a decision to do something about what she thought at the time was her inability to focus.

Maria started working with a Cognitive Behavioural Therapist who suggested a mindfulness course. Very soon, within a month, Maria began to notice a difference in her ability to concentrate.

Now, Maria had a better understanding of rumination. She could see how it was pulling her away from the present. She had learned to notice when she began to ruminate, and she would bring herself to the present moment using her breath, allowing her thought process to pass in its own time.

Example:

Phil was a personal trainer who was very organised and often joked about being a little OCD with clients who were late. Phil would state very clearly in his introductions that if people were late to a session then they would have to do 20 extra reps of whatever exercise he chose.

Whenever Phil was in the gym, waiting for clients to arrive, he would often experience automatic thoughts popping into his mind.

'Is she going to be late?' 'I can't afford for my sessions to run over.' 'What if he doesn't turn up?' 'He's always late he doesn't respect me.' 'She's doing it on purpose, I don't care if her son was ill'.

This began to affect the way his clients felt about Phil, and some clients asked to change trainers and others still, changed gyms, just to avoid the military style precision that Phil greeted and berated them with.

The manager of the gym asked to speak with Phil and after a rather heated debate about how important it was to be on time, the manager asked Phil to leave as he couldn't afford to lose anymore clients.

Once Phil had calmed down, he reflected on things and realised that he should consider getting some help to improve his customer service skills. He looked online and discovered lots of blog posts speaking about OCD and anxiety and what he could do to manage his thought patterns and resulting behaviours.

Phil is still working on himself, but now he realises, that when these thoughts pop into his head, they increase his anxiety and make him rather short tempered, and a little too brusque with clients.

After a sit down and long conversation with his old manager, Phil got his old job back and is doing much better with his client relationships.

OK, it's time to get personal. Here's an exercise to help you look at your own triggers and thought patterns.

Exercise:

What is my trigger?

....

....

....

What are some of the typical thoughts I have when this trigger comes up?

....

....

....

....

What are the automatic thoughts that pop up?

....

....

....

What do I ruminate on when this trigger comes up?

....

....

....

What good reasons exist for disregarding these thoughts?

....

....

....

What effect does ignoring or disregarding these thoughts have on my mood?

....

....

Repeat this exercise for all of the triggers you're aware of. Make sure to notice the difference between your automatic thoughts and the rumination.

Get into the practice of noticing anxious thoughts.

As you do so, it'll become easier to question all of your thoughts and choose carefully which ones you'll accept and which ones you'll dismiss.

Being more mindful and observant of your thoughts is something we will discuss further in the chapter on mindfulness.

8

WORKING WITH ANXIOUS
THOUGHTS

Our minds are full of thoughts. We love to think. It is what the mind was created to do. While we cannot stop ourselves from thinking, we can influence our thoughts.

Let's explore some of the most common thinking mistakes human beings tend to make.

You probably don't regularly make all of these thinking errors, but to help you better understand them, we invite you to imagine thinking in the ways described in the examples here.

Catastrophising is when you take a relatively minor event and imagine all sorts of terrors and nightmare scenarios resulting from it.

Another way of describing this thinking error is 'making a mountain out of a molehill'.

Imagine that you said something to offend your future mother-in-law.

If catastrophising, you'd jump to the conclusion that she'll turn your fiancée against you, the wedding will be off, your parents will be mortified, and nobody will ever want to go out with you again.

You might not even be aware that you're doing it. Next time you find yourself feeling as if the world is ending, answer the following questions:

What, if any, hard evidence supports my conclusions:

....

....

....

What, if any, hard evidence disproves my conclusions:

....

....

....

Can I adopt a more accurate perspective on the event?

....

....

....

What are some less terrible conclusions I can make about the event?

....

....

What practical steps can I take to deal with the situation?

....

....

....

....

All or nothing thinking – also called 'black or white' thinking. This involves assuming that a situation is entirely good or entirely bad, leaving no in-between or grey areas.

Say you went to a job interview and answered one question poorly. If you're thinking in an 'all or nothing' manner, you may decide that the entire interview was a complete wash out based on your one mistake.

Here's some questions to ask yourself, to help gain a different perspective:

- Am I focusing on only one aspect of the overall event?
- Am I giving one aspect of the event too much importance?
- What is a fair and accurate rating to give this aspect of the event on a scale of one to ten?

Demand Thinking - making demands is a big thinking error.

When you make demands you are expecting yourself, others, and the world to follow your rules and to never break them.

We all hold attitudes, values, standards, ideals, and beliefs about how the world and everyone in it ideally should act. And holding these opinions is all fine and well as long as we can be flexible and allow room for error and deviation.

But if you start demanding that everyone and everything sing to your tune, you'll be stressed and emotionally disturbed when things don't go your way.

Example:

Imagine that you have a preference to be treated politely. So, you tell yourself something like, 'I want to be treated politely but I don't absolutely have to be treated this way. I can stand a bit of impolite behaviour.'

Now imagine that you turn this preference into a demand. So, you tell yourself something like, 'I must be treated politely, and I can't stand it if I'm not!'

Can you see how the preference allows you to deal with impolite behaviour from others without leading to unhealthy anger?

Can you see how creating a demand may give rise to unhealthy anger and other unhealthy negative emotions?

Make your life better by being more flexible in your thinking. Here's some questions to answer to help you begin the process.

- What kind of language am I using in my head?
- Am I using terms such as 'must' or 'have to'?
- Am I accepting that other people have their own rules and can use their own free will?
- Is it possible for me to have my own high standards, but to also allow myself and others to fall short of these standards?
- Is my demand realistic?
- Is my demand ultimately helping me?
- How can I keep my standards and ideals, but turn my demands into preferences?

Fortune-telling this is making predictions about the future. You may firmly believe that your prophetic visions are correct.

The trouble is that many of your predictions are likely to be negative. They may even stop you from taking goal-directed action.

Example:

You want to approach your boss for a pay rise but predict that he'll say 'no' and be unpleasant about it. If you listen to your fortune-telling thoughts, you may never just take your chances and ask!

Challenge your predictions for the future by answering the questions below:

My prediction:

....

....

How can I test out my prediction?

....

....

....

What can I gain by risking taking action despite my negative prediction?

....

....

....

What events from my past may be influencing the way I expect this future event to unfold?

....

....

....

What action can I take to help myself adjust to a poor outcome? What steps can I take to try and resolve potential problems?

....

....

....

We do love to guess what others are thinking! But, when you mind-read, you often assume that others are thinking in judgemental and disapproving ways about you. These assumptions can lead to all sorts of difficulties, such as social anxiety and relationship ruptures.

Ask yourself how you can believe the best in this situation, rather than imagining the worst.

Now let's take a look at **mind reading** – that is, when you assume that you know what others are thinking about you, but have no evidence to support your thoughts.

Exercise:

Imagine that you go to a party with a friend and you don't know anyone there. Some people talk to you but then move on to talk to other people they seem to know.

You are on your own for a time and notice other people glancing at you. You assume that they're thinking 'who is she?', 'who invited her?', 'what in the world is she doing here?'.

Try questioning your mind-reading thoughts, before letting your thoughts run riot;

- What are some alternative explanations for my assumptions?
- Is it possible that my mind-reading may be wrong?
- What can I do to test out my mind-reading and gather more information?

Emotional reasoning is when you decide that your strong feelings are a true reflection of what is actually going on in reality. Because you feel a certain way you decide that your feelings must be correct. You then fail to take in other information that contradicts your feelings.

Example:

You feel very jealous about your partner's attention to another person. Because you feel so jealous, you may assume that your partner is definitely having an affair.

If you wake up in the morning feeling very anxious, you may assume that there must be something to be afraid of and look for a reason to be worried.

If emotional reasoning is one of your personal thinking errors, practice looking beyond your feelings. Consciously and deliberately put your feelings to one side. Use your observation skills to take in the reality of the situation.

Your feelings are more likely to reflect your own thoughts about what an event means to you than to reliably describe what is actually going on.

Begin to separate the facts from your feelings, by answering these questions below:

- What is the event or situation?
- What emotion am I experiencing?
- How might my feelings be leading me to distort the facts?
- What facts may I be ignoring because of my strong feelings?
- If I give myself time for my feelings to subside before drawing conclusions , how do I view the situation when I'm feeling calmer?

Over-generalising is a very common thinking pattern.

Do you find yourself thinking in terms of 'never' or 'always'? As in 'things *never* go my way' or 'I *always* screw up important meetings'? Or perhaps you think in global terms like 'people can't be trusted' or 'the world is unfair'?

Maybe you conclude that you're a totally bad parent, partner, employee, or whatever, based on one or more of your actions. Doing so can lead you to make some pretty rash and harsh judgements and to hold a pretty unforgiving attitude.

It's easy to allow a few bad things to cloud our judgement about an overall event or situation. Instead of deciding that something is all bad because of a few hiccups, try reminding yourself to keep the good stuff in sight.

Example:

You've recently started a new job. On your third day at work your boss presents you with a list of objectives, some of which you think are a bit unrealistic. You try to run the list past a few of your colleagues for some feedback but they're all too busy to talk.

You find yourself thinking that you always end up with totally unreasonable bosses, the job is terrible, and everyone you work with is unsupportive. You never get the good jobs.

You can stop yourself over-generalising by being highly specific about the negative aspects of a particular situation,

- What is the specific thing I am basing my judgements on?
- Am I making a total judgement of myself, others, or a situation based on this one specific aspect?
- What other aspects of myself, others, or the situation am I ignoring?
- Can I suspend total judgement and instead judge only the specific aspect of myself, others, or the situation?
- How might I benefit from being more specific in my judgement?

Labelling and rating or categorizing can cause major emotional distress. You fail an exam, and you label yourself a failure. You take one characteristic of yourself or another person, and apply it across the board to everything they do.

So, you call yourself, other people, and the world nasty names. If you call yourself 'useless' every time you screw up, or the world 'cruel' every time it deals you a blow, or others 'no good' when you're treated impolitely, then you're in danger of feeling a lot of really toxic emotions.

Example:

Your friend has recently had a bereavement. You can't go to visit her on Friday night because you have prior plans.

When you next speak to her she sounds very low and a bit annoyed with you for failing to visit. You then label yourself as a totally selfish person and a rubbish friend because you didn't put her needs first on Friday night.

Try giving up the rating game. Use the questions below to see yourself and others as more complex than your labels may suggest.

- What is the label I apply to myself or others?
- Am I being fair when I apply this label?
- Am I allowing for varying degrees of goodness or badness in myself, others, or the world?
- What are some other more complex aspects of this person, myself, or the situation that I may be overlooking when I apply a label?
- Is it possible for me to label the specific action or event instead of the whole person, myself, or the world?

With **Mental Filtering** you only let information through that fits with what you already believe about yourself, others, or the world.

If you think of yourself as a failure you only process information that points to you failing; and if you think the world is unsafe. then you only acknowledge scary and dangerous news about the world.

This filtering process can lead you to have a very biased and negative view of yourself and your environment.

Pretend for a moment that you believe that the world is a dangerous and unpleasant place. You fail to take in articles about successful recycling initiatives, crime reduction in major cities, and elderly people being entertained by youth groups.

Tackle this thinking error by letting in additional information that contradicts your viewpoint. Answer the questions below to help you organise your thoughts.

- What is my particular filter?
- What information is my filter stopping me from considering?
- How might I think and behave if I were to remove my filter?

Disqualifying the positive is very similar to mental filtering.

Imagine, for example, that you believe that you are unlikable and unacceptable socially. Your mental filter only lets you notice information that supports your negative self-opinion.

If any positive information does sneak through your filter, you quickly discredit or disqualify it and throw it back out.

Example:

You believe you are fundamentally unlikable. Someone asks you to go for a drink after work. Instead of seeing the invitation as evidence against your idea that you're unlikable, you may think that they're only asking you because nobody else was available or because they feel sorry for you.

The questions below help you counteract this thinking bias by deliberately and consistently gathering *positive* data.

- How do I respond to positive cues from others and my environment?
- Do I acknowledge positive feedback and respond to it?
- What positive information and experiences can I write down? (I can look at my positive data log when I find myself thinking negatively.)

- How can I practise taking a compliment graciously?
- How will acknowledging positive information from others help me?

Having **Low Frustration Tolerance** (LFT) is about deciding that uncomfortable equals unbearable.

Basically, if you have LFT, you're likely to give up striving toward your goals whenever the going gets too tough or painful.

The adage that anything worth having requires effort and is worth the blood, sweat, and tears really does hold true. A lot of good things in life don't come easily.

Imagine you want to improve your health by losing a few pounds and getting fit through exercise. But as soon as you're offered a cream cake you tell yourself that resisting it is too painful and the deprivation is unbearable.

You go to the gym but as soon as your muscles begin to ache you decide that you just can't take the discomfort and exercise is too much like hard work. So, you go home, order a pizza, and flake out in front of the telly.

Overcome low frustration tolerance by challenging your attitude toward discomfort and by fostering high frustration tolerance.

Here's some questions to ask yourself.

- Is what I'm experiencing really intolerable and unbearable?
- Is what I'm experiencing really just difficult to tolerate or to bear?
- What are some of the reasons that make bearing this discomfort worthwhile?
- What evidence exists to support the idea that I can tolerate this discomfort?

- What other things worth doing can I push myself to do, even if they're uncomfortable or unpleasant?

Personalising involves taking random events and making them a personal issue. You tend to make everything that happens around you about you, even if reality indicates otherwise. This tendency can lead you to assume inappropriate responsibility for events and/or to feel unhealthy emotions in response to events that have little or nothing to do with you.

Example:

You plan a barbecue and invite your neighbours. Unfortunately, a freak thunderstorm rolls in just as the burgers are on the grill. Several women rush home because their clothes are sodden.

One couple starts arguing. In the end, the remaining guests and your family sit down to potato salad in your kitchen, whilst the barbecue pit outside gently smoulders.

You think that the weather is out to get you, the women are holding you to blame for their ruined outfits, and clearly your aborted barbecue has resulted in the impending divorce of the rowing couple.

You can remove yourself from the centre of the universe and take things less personally by challenging your thoughts and being more objective.

Here's some questions to ask yourself:

- What else has contributed to the outcome of the situation, other than you?
- Are you taking personal responsibility for things that are not within your control?
- What are some additional reasons that may account for the way people around you are responding?
- Are you really the only person affected by specific events and conditions, or are others affected too?

- Is what has happened really all about you?

In this chapter we've tried to identify the types of anxious thoughts you experience. We've given you some tools to handle them.

If this chapter contains some things that you struggle with, read or listen to that part of the chapter again, making notes on the actions that you can take.

9

WORRY AND ANXIETY

Whatever type of anxiety you suffer from, the chances are that worry is also a big part of your life.

We're led to believe that worrying is a normal part of life and almost a rite of passage to adulthood.

However, when worry becomes paralysing and feeds into your anxiety, creating unwanted thoughts, emotions and behaviours, then worry has out stayed it's welcome.

Let's be clear, we'll probably never eliminate all worry, just as it isn't possible to eliminate our thoughts. In order to avoid worry all together, you'd have to not care about anything.

There's a world of difference between healthy concern and unhealthy anxiety. The latter involves unproductive worry. Worry takes up a lot of time and energy. It's unproductive, and feeds anxiety.

If you notice that your current most pressing worries tend to recur time and again albeit in slightly different forms, then you have some definite worry themes. This means that you probably tend to worry about certain areas of your life too much, even when nothing is going wrong.

Common worry themes include:

- finances
- health
- relationships
- work or career
- business
- family
- other people's opinions of you.

The exercise at the end of this chapter has been created to help you understand that you may have a worry problem more than you have actual problems. In other words, whether the process of worrying is what's causing you the most anxiety.

Worrying is a habit that, with persistence and the help of CBT, you can break.

You may feel strange and even vulnerable when you first start resisting your worry habit. With time you'll get used to the awesome relief of no longer being a constant worrier. Doing so takes a lot of hard work but the result is definitely worth it.

Work your way out of your worry maze with this exercise.

Exercise:

Let's try this exercise, by asking some questions about whatever it is that you're currently worrying about:

What is your current worry?

....

....

....

Is this worry an actual problem?

....

....

Is this something that I can work to solve today?

....

....

If yes, what practical actions can you take to solve the problem?

Write down your answers below:

Step 1:

....

....

....

Step 2:

....

....

....

Step 3:

....

....

....

Step 4:

....

....

....

Step 5:

....

....

....

If not, then you've established that there's nothing you can do right now. What activities can you turn my attention to instead of focusing on my worrying thoughts?

Write down your suggestions below:

1.

....

....

2.

....

....

3.

....

....

4.

....

....

5.

....

....

Remind yourself that worrying does nothing to prevent or solve problems, it simply feeds anxiety. You can manage and negotiate life just fine, minus the worry.

10

EXPLORING ANXIOUS EMOTIONS

Many CBT therapists make a distinction between two types of negative feeling states or emotions – healthy emotions and unhealthy emotions.

Healthy emotions are those feelings you have in response to negative events that are appropriate to the event, lead to constructive action, and don't significantly interfere with the rest of your life.

Unhealthy emotions are feelings you have that are out of proportion to the event in question. Unhealthy emotions tend to lead to self-destructive behaviours, and cause problems in other areas of your life.

One of the key objectives of CBT is to help you to experience healthy negative emotions safely and with less fear.

It's helpful to begin by identifying your feelings and emotions. As therapists, we can use lots of different words to describe subtly different emotions.

You may be more accustomed to using vague terms to articulate how you feel inside. Perhaps you use words such as 'upset', 'worked up', or 'bad'.

If you're using these words, that's an indication that you're in a negative emotional state, but they don't really provide much more information beyond that.

It's important to learn to distinguish between the different types of negative emotions.

A good example of this would be John and how he managed to process the grief following the death of his father.

Example:

John often struggles with first identifying and then regulating his emotions since the death of his father a year ago. Before this John was a rather jovial man who enjoyed social interaction and was known for his loud belly laugh and warm nature.

John didn't seek any help or support from professionals after his father passed. As the oldest son he felt he had to be strong for his elderly mother, who was now a widow, and take care of all of the funeral arrangements with a little help from his younger siblings.

Now after many months of missing his father, who was his best friend and fishing partner, John is struggling to express his emotions and often finds himself yelling at loved ones or completely shutting down.

John's wife eventually sought grief counselling for John and his siblings, and John is now learning to face his emotions. Where John had often felt that he was now very 'angry' at the loss of his father, he began to identify the full range of emotions associated with his father's passing.

John is often frustrated when he remembers that he was at work when his father collapsed. Although he couldn't have prevented his passing, he wishes that he had been able to get to him faster and maybe he could have helped.

John also often feels disappointed that he wasn't able to mourn his father properly when he first passed. Even though he wanted to be strong for his family, he felt as if there was something wrong with him that he couldn't cry until many months later.

At other times John is simply very sad at the loss of his role model, advisor and friend in life. He looked up to his father, had a great deal of respect for him and misses him dearly.

By learning how to first identify and then label his emotions, recognising the subtle yet important differences, John is better able to manage his behaviours. As a result his grieving process is well underway, and his relationships are much improved.

By the end of this chapter you will also have learnt how to:

- Expand your emotional vocabulary so you know what you're feeling
- Identify that an emotion is going on
- Know exactly what the emotion is
- Understand why the emotion is present
- Have a technical label for that 'stomach churning feeling'
- Be able to put a name to your emotions faster and easier than before

The three main advantages to applying a specific label or name to your feelings are that:

- It is easier for others (and even for yourself) to understand the precise nature of what you're feeling.
- It makes it easier for you to work out whether what you're feeling is a healthy or unhealthy negative emotion.
- It becomes easier for you to select an alternative healthy negative emotion as a goal.

There are three basic steps to identifying or naming your emotions:

1. One way of giving a name to your feelings is to begin by

noting what triggered your feelings. The trigger or event that starts your emotional juices flowing can give a strong indication of the exact feeling.

2. Look closely at how your emotion leads you to act, or want to act we call these action tendencies.

3. Make your emotional guess as you unravel what you're feeling and decide on what label or name to give to your emotional experience.

If you still find the process of naming emotions difficult, don't worry. Sometimes what you need are more feeling words at your fingertips.

Here's a list of common human emotions. You can refer to this list whenever you want inspiration or are at a loss for words describing your current emotional state.

- Anger
- Anxiety
- Concern
- Depression
- Disappointment
- Embarrassment
- Envy
- Fear
- Grief
- Guilt
- Hurt
- Jealousy
- Regret
- Remorse
- Sadness
- Shame

This is by no means a conclusive list. Bear in mind that, as you learn more words, perhaps with a dictionary or thesaurus, you can add them to your list here.

All human emotions – whether positive or negative, healthy or unhealthy – are triggered by thoughts. Once you learn to identify your emotions you will have the ability to choose how to manage both your thoughts and emotions.

Spend some time now going through various scenario's and finding the correct word or label to describe your emotion at the time.

Exercise: Identifying Emotions

Scenario/Event:

....

....

Trigger:

....

....

Thoughts and images:

....

....

Physical sensations and changes:

....

....

Emotion(s):

....

....

You can use the following example to help you explore your own emotions.

Example:

Sandra had only been married for 18 months when she found out she was pregnant with her first child. Her husband was delighted, and they couldn't wait to share the good news with family and friends.

Unfortunately, at 14 weeks, Sandra suffered a miscarriage and as a result, completely withdrew from her regular life.

She couldn't fully understand what her emotions were. At the time she just felt very sad and what she described as depressed.

Sandra was unmotivated, she didn't want to speak to family and friends and she pushed her husband away every time he tried to console her.

Here are the results of Sandra's Identifying Emotions Exercise:

- Scenario/Event: Going to the supermarket
- Trigger: Seeing a new born baby in a pram
- Thoughts and images: That should have been me and my baby, images of her unborn baby how the pram she had picked out would look.
- Physical sensations and changes: Churning stomach, head ache, confusion and a desire to leave the supermarket quickly
- Emotions: Envy, sadness, grief.

Now, go back to the exercise above. Spend some time thinking of your own scenario and what the actual emotions are that appear.

11

―――――――――――――

HOW OUR EMOTIONS WORK

Our emotions don't exist in a self-contained bubble. Human emotions exist in context.

All human emotions – whether positive or negative, healthy or unhealthy – are comprised of four dimensions.

The following four dimensions interact and reinforce one another:

1. *Thoughts* – thinking patterns and thoughts will trigger emotions
2. *Attention* – what you pay the most attention to, will affect your emotions
3. *Focus* – where you place your focus affects your emotions
4. *Behaviour* – the actions you take will affect how you feel.

In addition to these dimensions, some of your physical sensations are also ways of determining whether you're in the grip of an healthy or an unhealthy emotional experience.

These four aspects or dimensions of emotional experience are different depending on the type of feeling you're having.

For example, the *action tendencies* associated with healthy sadness tend to be constructive. They help you to accept and adjust to a negative event or situation.

Example:

In the case of Johns father passing, when he accepted that part of the grieving process is to feel and express sadness, it helped him to accept his father's passing and he could move forward through the grieving process.

The action tendencies associated with unhealthy sadness tend to be destructive, because they prevent you from accepting the negative event and moving forward.

Example:

When Sandra refused to speak to family and friends and even her husband, who was also grieving, she dwelled in her sadness.

Sandra couldn't cope with seeing young mums and their newborn babies in the supermarket. This created a negative reaction, bringing up feelings of envy, intense sadness and grief.

In general, healthy negative emotions are less intensely uncomfortable than their unhealthy counterparts. Even if you're extremely sad, you're likely to feel less intense discomfort or emotional pain than if you're unhealthily anxious.

Rigid thinking is a sure-fire sign that you're feeling something unhealthy.

An example of **rigid thinking** involves demanding that you, others, and the world play by certain rules – your rules.

This attitude is troublesome because you leave no room for deviation or error. So, when your demands aren't met, and they frequently won't be, you're likely to become emotionally disturbed.

Example:

Sandra was caught in the trap of rigid thinking, not being able to face the reality of the miscarriage. She demanded that people not speak to her about the event and also refused to deal with her emotions in a healthy way.

The alternative to rigid/demand-based thinking is *flexible* or *preference-based thinking.*

Here, you hold preferences, standards, and ideals for how you, others, and the world perform. But – and the but is crucial – you also accept the possibility of your preferences *not* being met.

In this way, when you fail to live up to your personal standards, others behave in undesirable ways, or the world refuses to fall in with your plans, you may feel emotionally distressed, but not unduly disturbed.

Example:

A good example of this would be how John engaged in counselling after his wife took steps to find someone that could help him with his grief.

Although it wasn't his choice initially, he was open to finding out more about what was happening and seeking a solution, as to why he hadn't been able to mourn his father.

The counselling didn't solve all of his problems. He was still emotionally distressed, but he did learn a new approach to grieving and managing his emotions.

When you hold onto demands that aren't met, you're also at risk of putting yourself or others down harshly. Doing so can lead to more emotional pain and more practical problems too.

Look out for words and phrases such as 'should', 'must', 'it's essential', 'have to', 'got to', and 'ought to' in your thinking and self-talk. These are often signs that you're thinking rigidly.

Being aware of your behaviour

Our emotions dictate our behaviour to a large extent. By acknowledging the ways we act when we're emotionally charged up, we can further determine the relative health of your feelings.

Here's some of the typical behaviours that tend to go hand-in-hand with healthy and unhealthy emotions.

We also call our behaviours '*action tendencies*' because you may feel like you want to act in a certain way but not actually do it.

Take a look at the list below of *emotions* and the related *action tendencies* and see what difference you notice.

Healthy Emotions

Here's some healthy emotions - read through the list and see if any might apply to you:

- Annoyance or anger
- Concern
- Sadness
- Benign envy
- Remorse
- Disappointment
- Benign jealousy

Action Tendencies

These healthy emotions can trigger certain actions. These may include some of the following:

- Asserting yourself in a respectful but firm manner. Not becoming abusive or violent. Being willing to consider the other person's point of view.
- Facing up to threats. Seeking a reasonable amount of reassurance.
- After a period of mourning and reflection, reinvesting in the

company of others. Carrying on with meaningful or enjoyed activities.

- Striving to gain what another has that you desire but don't have.
- Allowing others to enjoy what they have without trying to spoil it for them.
- Admitting that you want what they have.
- Asking for forgiveness and facing up to the person you have wronged.
- Taking the correct amount of responsibility for the wrongdoing.
- Voicing your feelings.
- Giving the other person a chance to explain or apologise. Being willing to make the first move.
- Asking honest and straightforward questions.
- Being open minded.

You can see from this list there are a variety of healthy action tendencies that you can adopt when you're experiencing strong emotions.

In the same way that John voiced his feelings, and managed after a period of mourning and reflection, to reinvest in the company of others, you can too.

Unhealthy Emotions

Here's some unhealthy emotions - read through the list and see if any are familiar to you:

- Anger or rage
- Anxiety
- Depression
- Acidic envy
- Guilt
- Hurt

- Acidic jealousy

Action Tendencies

These unhealthy emotions can trigger certain actions. These may include some of the following:

- Shouting, being violent and abusive, putting the other person down. Insisting that you're right.
- Avoiding threat.
- Seeking excessive reassurance.
- Withdrawing from social reinforcements and meaningful or enjoyed activities.
- Self-isolating.
- Spoiling another's enjoyment of what you want, but don't have.
- Sour grapes.
- Pretending you don't really want what they have.
- Begging forgiveness from, or avoiding facing, the person you have wronged.
- Taking too much responsibility for the wrongdoing.
- Sulking.
- Trying to hint at what the other person has done wrong, so they have to make the first move.
- Being suspicious.
- Spying or checking up on another person.
- Questioning them and setting tests for them.

Example:

As you can see from this list, Sandra is taking too much responsibility for what has happened. She is self-isolating, pretending she doesn't want what she see's new mothers have, and withdrawing from social reinforcements and meaningful activities.

If you recognise some or any of these action tendencies in yourself, then consider what you can do to move closer to the behaviours in the first list.

Bear in mind that you can use any word you like to describe your actual emotions. Just make sure that you use a different term for your healthy emotion and the unhealthy alternative.

Once you're able to identify your emotions as healthy or unhealthy, your next step is to decide which unhealthy emotions you want to target for change.

These are probably the emotions you experience most often or those that interfere most significantly with the smooth running of your life.

Unhealthy - Healthy Emotion

Here are some examples of how you can move from an unhealthy emotion to a healthy one.

As you read through the list, make a mental note of those which you feel apply most to you.

- Anxiety - - - > concern
- Depression - - - > sadness
- Acidic envy - - - > - benign envy
- Guilt - - - > remorse
- Hurt - - - > disappointment
- Acidic jealousy - - - > - benign jealousy
- Rage - - - > annoyance
- Shame -- - - > regret

Now take some time to identify your key emotions and find the unhealthy and healthy options for them.

Which unhealthy emotions do you want to target for change?

12

MINDFULNESS AND CBT

CBT involves dealing with the content of your thoughts, your feelings and emotions and your actions or behaviours.

However, CBT also recognises some more recent developments in therapy, such as mindfulness.

In fact, CBT principles have been integrated to create an entirely new wave of therapy called MBCT - Mindfulness Based Cognitive Therapy.

While we will not be delving into MBCT within this book, let's take a look at mindfulness meditation and how it can be used as a tool to help you become less reactive and reduce anxiety, worry and stress.

Mindfulness is the practice of being aware without judgement. This practice encourages us to simply accept our thoughts without trying to change them, take any action or avoid them.

Put simply, there are times when your thoughts are best left alone. By accepting unwelcome thoughts and essentially allowing them to play themselves out without any interruption or intervention on your part, you can practice exposure to unpleasant thoughts, images, or physical sensations.

If you're able to accept your thoughts as just thoughts, rather than interpreting them as facts, you can lessen their emotional impact.

Let's take a look at some basic mindfulness exercises that you can use to help you better manage troublesome thoughts, images, and negative physical feelings or emotions.

Exercise: Focussed Attention

The whole experience of mindfulness is like looking at the world with fresh eyes, free from judgement or comment.

The idea is to hold your attention in the present moment and to focus as much as possible on the here and now.

This may sound very simple, in practice, though, this it takes time to master. Don't be too hard on yourself if it takes a while for you to grasp the idea.

Our minds are used to thinking about past events or worrying about the future.

When you notice your mind beginning to wander into worry territory or to planning your next move, gently bring it back to the here and now. Choose to refocus your mind on what is happening in the present moment.

Continue to focus as much as you can on whatever you are currently doing. Don't dwell on the past or concern yourself with the future.

Example:

If you are brushing your teeth, focus your attention on the actual experience of brushing your teeth.

If you're walking, focus on the sights and sounds around you, as well as the physical sensations of your body as it moves.

If you are sitting in a chair, then focus on how your body feels sitting in the chair. Breathe in deeply, then slowly exhale. Focus on the feelings and sounds of your breathing. Continue for 3-5 minutes , then carry on with your day.

Exercise: Suspending judgement

Most of the time we make snap judgements about our experiences without even being completely aware of doing so.

This way we label our experiences as good, bad, or neutral.

By trying this simple mindfulness exercise, you can practice suspending judgement and simply accept experiences for what they are, experiences.

Try to focus your attention on whatever you're doing – be it gardening, waiting in a queue, or eating a meal.

Instead of judging an event as good, bad, boring, or satisfying, try to experience the moment fully without making any value judgements about it.

Suspending judgement can be very useful for dealing with unwelcome thoughts and feelings.

Rather than judging your thoughts and feelings as bad, try to accept their presence and don't attach any value or meaning to them.

Exercise: The Thought Train

Let's explore another mindfulness technique. The thought train is a technique to help you manage unhelpful thoughts.

It requires you to simply allow your thoughts to pass by. Imagine your thoughts and feelings as carriages on a train.

Rather than trying to control or stop unwelcome thoughts or think more about them, simply just observe them.

Instead of engaging with your thoughts, watch them pass through the station and carry on down the track.

Resist the urge to jump on the thought train and instead just let it chug on by.

Notice how difficult it is and how often you feel the urge to jump on board. With time and plenty of practice this will become easier.

Practicing Mindfulness

Mindfulness and meditation have great power when it comes to exploring the mind and the soul, and especially when it comes to being more aware of both yourself and your surroundings.

Mindfulness is all about awareness.

Meditation can help you focus on the present moment, reducing those thoughts about the past and worries about the future.

It is about reaching a state of being completely present in the moment – and it is also about using that awareness to think calmly over everything that is happening.

In turn, you get an opportunity to look at things from a different perspective.

You start to see solutions to common problems more clearly. And, of course, you are able to start addressing challenging obstacles and roadblocks in your life, without becoming overwhelmed with events, and without overreacting.

Why not make a note to practice some of the above mindfulness exercises regularly?

The Power of Meditation

Meditation is a simple technique, but you need to practice, as it is also a skill that you can learn and improve upon.

There are a few ways that you can improve your experience, by following a couple of tips that ensure you can meditate and feel relaxed and calm afterward.

Firstly, even though you need to keep your mind collected, understand that it is okay for your mind to wander now and again.

When this happens, go with the flow. See where your mind takes you. Judge the thought lightly, but don't judge yourself or your mind for wandering off.

Once you have done this, it's important to bring your mind back to what you were focusing on and to re-enter your state of meditation.

As you meditate, be sure to try and reach a level of awareness where you completely acknowledge all that is happening.

Understand your surroundings, know exactly what situation you are in. Tell yourself everything will be alright, because you can make the right decision when you are calm. Let your negative thoughts fly away.

When it comes to meditation, practice really does make perfect, as the technique is a skill.

We all possess the basic human abilities to be aware and to achieve that level of self-awareness that mindfulness and meditation techniques are able to bring to us, but we need to practice how to harness these skills and make the most out of them.

Only through regular practice sessions will you truly start to improve your ability to closely focus your mind on yourself and reach that level of awareness that will grant you complete power over your thoughts, as well as your mind.

When you achieve this level, you'll start to experience significant benefits. Calming your mind becomes easy and relaxing after a stressful situation becomes something you can do in just a few minutes, even when the next stressful event is about to happen.

As you progress and improve your ability to be mindful, you'll eventually be able to start practicing these techniques in ways that do not necessarily require you to sit down in a peaceful and comfortable position.

You'll be able to clear your mind, while you are in the middle of that stressful moment, and things will start to become clearer to you.

You'll notice things that you missed before, because you are gaining a new perspective of the issue at hand, and allowing yourself the ability to better solve whatever life, your career, or anything else might throw your way.

If you struggle to find time for meditation during your day, consider listening to a guided meditation as you fall asleep. You'll find links to some guided meditations in the final chapter.

Listening to a guided meditation can help reduce anxiety and clear your mind, preparing you for a restful night and good sound sleep.

13

CAN THE FUTURE BE BRIGHT AGAIN?

This is a question that many people are thinking and perhaps are afraid to ask.

It may seem like almost too much to ask that one day you will feel as if you have a bright future ahead.

The truth is that no matter how old you are, how severe your anxiety or how dark your days have been, there is hope. One day your future *can* be bright again.

You've probably been living according to your unhealthy core beliefs for many years, maybe most of your life. The fact that you automatically experience unhealthy thinking, when you encounter a negative life event, is therefore understandable.

With the help of CBT, the good news is that these habits and patterns can be broken.

It may not be easy at first. You'll have to work at it, but with time, effort and lots of practice, you will begin to notice improvements and a difference in your everyday life.

Over time your brain adjusts to your altered circumstances and before you know it you're doing things relatively easily.

We've covered a lot about the idea behind CBT and how you can learn to change your unhelpful thought patterns. You've learned a huge amount and now you're ready to get yourself a new set of healthy beliefs, that you are ready to work on and strengthen.

Learning to live with a new set of beliefs will take work. You'll need to re-program your brain to make sense of situations in a new way.

Our unhelpful core beliefs tend to be very rigid and long held. Daily persistence, practice and patience are needed, until one day it all falls into place and you find yourself operating under your new set of core beliefs.

Most people who practice CBT can recognise the self-defeating nature of their unhealthy beliefs. They figure out, with the help and support of a therapist or workbook, better ways of thinking, and understand that their new beliefs make sense.

However, it's not uncommon to hear patients say, 'I know these new beliefs will help me, but I just don't really believe them yet.' If that sounds like you right now, it sounds like your heart and your heart are in conflict.

That's OK, it's perfectly normal. In fact, in CBT, it's referred to as 'what you know to be true and helpful and what you actually believe', the 'head-heart' or 'head-gut' issue.

The following chapters are devoted to helping you resolve the 'head-heart' conflict.

14

CORE BELIEFS

Our past experiences and early childhood situations can influence the way we think about ourself and others and how we make sense of the world in our present life.

We learn certain messages from our parents, our relatives, teachers, and peers. Sometimes these messages are helpful and other times they are not.

As we get older, we often reassess the validity and usefulness of some of our early beliefs and ideas.

However, there are some ideas we took as gospel truth in our early life. We don't re-evaluate them, and continue to live according to these philosophies and beliefs.

In CBT, these long-standing enduring beliefs about yourself, people, or the world are called *core beliefs*. Core beliefs are generally global and absolute in nature.

It's likely that you consider that your core beliefs are 100 per cent true at all times. You may ignore or misinterpret evidence that contradicts them.

If you think of core beliefs as being at the very heart of your belief system – and the way you understand yourself and all the things around you – you can begin to see how important they are to your mental and emotional health.

Core beliefs fall into three main camps:

1. *Beliefs about yourself* inform the way you understand your own worth. If you experienced harsh criticism, neglect or abuse as a child, you may have learnt to think of yourself as weak, unworthy or inadequate, for example.
2. *Your beliefs about other people* also frequently have their roots in early life. Again, if you suffered traumas or very negative treatment from others you may adopt the belief that people are dangerous or untrustworthy.
3. *Your beliefs about life* in general, and how the world operates, help determine your general attitudes. If you grew up in a deprived or unpredictable environment, you may develop negative beliefs about the world and life.

By definition, it's hard for you to be aware of your own core beliefs.

Here's an exercise you can use to help you understand more about your core beliefs.

Exercise: Existing Core Beliefs

Think about a recent situation or event that stirred up strong feelings. This could be related directly to anxiety, or simply an event like a dinner, day out, or revisiting a location you haven't been to for a while.

Once you have the scenario clearly in your mind, ask yourself these questions about that situation or event:

What are my immediate thoughts?

....

....

What are my personal rules and demands in this case?

....

....

What does this tell me about my core beliefs about myself?

....

....

What does this tell me about my core beliefs about others?

....

....

What does this tell me about my core beliefs about the world and life?

....

....

Provide full and detailed answers to all the following questions:

What does this tell me about my core beliefs about myself?

....

....

What does this tell me about my core beliefs about other people?

....

....

What does this tell me about my core beliefs about the world and life?

....

....

Try running through different scenario's, these can be recent or past events. Try to come up with the core beliefs that were operating at the time.

Example

Michael had moved away after University to pursue a career in the City of London as a Barrister. He had come from humble beginnings in Newcastle, where he was adopted by kind and loving working -class parents.

Michael studied hard and was now well on his way to being an International Counsel for large corporations around the world.

Michaels upbringing had been very challenging and as a result he avoids going home too often, preferring to 'treat' his parents to stays in fancy hotels and theatre nights in London's West End.

When Michael's adopted sister invited him back to Newcastle for her 50th Birthday party, he had no choice but to return home. Once Michael arrived, he had the time of his life. He met old school friends, extended family members who greeted him with open arms and more pints of beer than he could drink.

He laughed and joked about old times long into the night, and even as he returned to his hotel, he was filled with complete awe at the generosity of these people who welcomed him as if he had never left his home town.

Here are the answers from Michael's exercise:

What are my immediate thoughts? Oh no, it's going to be terrible, cold, dark, miserable and I'm going to have to buy all the drinks.

What are my personal rules and demands in this case? I will leave early, everyone has to respect me as a Barrister now, not little Mike. I won't stay with family, I'll book myself into the best hotel in town.

What does this tell me about my core beliefs about myself? That I am now very different from the boy who grew up here, my background isn't what made me who I am, I'm a self-made man. I have nothing in common with these people.

I am hard working and willing to go further than most others and have beaten the odds to become very successful.

What does this tell me about my core beliefs about others? That they haven't worked as hard as me to make something of themselves. If they stayed in Newcastle, they didn't have the drive to succeed and they don't understand me.

People are lazy and are waiting for a hand out and a helping hand to better themselves rather than doing the work.

What does this tell me about my core beliefs about the world/life? That you have to move far away from your humble beginnings if you want to be successful. That in order to make something of yourself, you have to change who were, if you were poor or working class.

Life can be hard but regardless of what background you come from as long as you work hard you can become successful.

Now take some time to go through the questions and answer them for yourself.

Go through this process for other recent situations and events, until you are satisfied that you've identified some of your core beliefs.

Once you've done this, move onto the next exercise to begin creating new core beliefs for yourself.

Creating New Core Beliefs

Re-imagining your core beliefs is an exercise that will require patience and a measure of reality.

This is not an exercise to create unrealistic beliefs, your beliefs must be rooted in reality. However, they can be more open in nature, less repressive towards yourself and others.

Most importantly, they can give you an element of freedom from the ever resent need to control, catastrophize or be certain.

Once you've identified your existing beliefs, you're ready to change your core beliefs, bringing them in line with a healthy thought life.

Remind yourself of positive experiences you've had with other people. Remember your own positive traits and characteristics that you like about yourself.

Focus on anything else that you've experienced, that suggests the world has good things to offer.

Healthy core beliefs have the following characteristics:

1. They are flexible, and preference-based. Instead of insisting that you must meet certain criteria, you *prefer* a specific outcome or desire to achieve a specific goal, but you also accept the possibility of failing to do so.

You leave room for normal human error and for random life events. So instead of 'I must not fail!' you may have the healthy belief 'I'd prefer not to fail', but there is no reason that I absolutely must not'.

2. They include a sensible if-then statement. Instead of concluding extreme negative things about yourself, others, or the world, based on a singular event, you can put the event into a healthy perspective.

So rather than 'If I fail at something, then it proves that I am a total failure', you may believe 'If I fail, then it's bad but not terrible and just means that I am a normal fallible person'.

3. They include a positive and realistic general truth. Rather than assigning global negative ratings to yourself, others or the world, you allow for the coexistence of good, less good, neutral, and bad elements.

So, in place of a belief such as 'I'm worthless' and 'the world is terrible,' you may have 'I am basically okay' or 'the world is complex and has both good and bad parts.'

Step 1

Make note of the beliefs that you want to take on board for each of three main categories:

- *Yourself*: Your self-opinion and ideas about your worthiness.
- *Other people*: Your view of others and how you expect them to behave generally or toward you specifically.
- *The world and life*: Your expectations of how the world will treat you, how life is likely to unfold for you and/or others.

Step 2

Now write down your new healthy beliefs being sure to express why they make sense, reflect reality and help you to function.

- *Yourself*: Your self-opinion and ideas about your worthiness.
- *Other people*: Your view of others and how you expect them to behave generally or toward you specifically.
- *The world and life*: Your expectations of how the world will treat you, how life is likely to unfold for you and/or others.

Make your beliefs hold to these basic guidelines:

- *True and consistent with reality:* Ensure that your new beliefs or philosophies don't distort the facts of any given situation or event, nor deny the actual situation or event.

- *Flexible and preference-based:* They leave a margin for error. They recognise that you and other humans are fallible, and capable of both success and failure at any given task or endeavour. They acknowledge that life is full of random events and that complete certainty is rarely possible.
- *Balanced and non-extreme:* You resist using judgemental, absolute, harsh labels to describe yourself, others, or the world. Instead strive to use descriptive terms that include the complexity and changeability of you, other people and life itself.
- *Sensible and logical:* Construct new beliefs that make good sense and are logically sound.
- *Helpful to you:* Your new beliefs should be ways of thinking that can assist you in reaching your goals and lead to mental and emotional health.

Example:

This is how Michael re-imagined his core belief about himself. This includes his beliefs about him being very hardworking, and others being lazy and not willing to make the sacrifices needed to be successful.

Step 1

Make note of the beliefs that you want to take on board for each of three main categories:

- *Yourself:* Your self-opinion and ideas about your worthiness.

I am hard working and willing to go further than most others and have beaten the odds to become very successful.

- *Other people:* Your view of others and how you expect them to behave generally or toward you specifically.

Most people are lazy and are waiting for a hand out and a helping hand to better themselves rather than doing the work.

- *The world and life*: Your expectations of how the world will treat you, how life is likely to unfold for you and/or others.

Life can be hard but regardless of what background you come from as long as you work hard you can become successful.

Step 2

Now write down your new healthy beliefs, being sure to express why they make sense, reflect reality and help you to function.

- *Yourself*: Your self-opinion and ideas about your worthiness.

I am a hard-worker, but part of my success is due to my upbringing. I was raised in an honest hardworking family, I knew I was adopted and was grateful for such loving and kind parents.

My parents influenced my decision to become a barrister and encouraged my self-belief. Although I was brought up in an environment where it was a little tougher than many, but it just made me more resilient.

- *Other people*: Your view of others and how you expect them to behave generally or toward you specifically.

My family and friends were very supportive of me, and in fact, if it wasn't for them, I might not have had the support I needed to get through the hard times.

It's nice when people treat you like family, just as when you were growing up it gives a sense of comfort and authenticity. I prefer people to be themselves, rather than act superficially as many people do in my life now.

The world and life: Your expectations of how the world will treat you, how life is likely to unfold for you and/or others.

Whatever cards life deals you, the love and support of good people will get you through. We all have a responsibility to help others, in the same way I was extended love, kindness and support my entire life.

It's time to take action and start working on your own core beliefs with the following exercise.

Exercise: Re-Imagining Core Beliefs

Let's begin by stating clearly one of your negative core beliefs.

This exercise will take some time, and you may want to return to it over a few days before you feel satisfied.

This will give you time to process your new ways of thinking, while also giving you the opportunity to develop your core beliefs according to the guidelines above.

Core Unhelpful Beliefs

Complete the following prompts:

I am:

....

....

The world is:

....

....

Other people:

....

....

Now re-imagine this core belief in a way that contradicts the original core belief.

New Core Belief

Complete the following prompts:

I am:

....

....

The world is:

....

....

Other people:

....

....

Now, go back through your new core beliefs and ask yourself the following questions. Are your new core beliefs:

- True and consistent
- Flexible
- Balanced, not extreme
- Logical
- Helpful to you?

In the light of your answers, go back and review your new core beliefs. Make changes until you feel happy with your answers.

15

LIFE STRATEGY

Living a full life is not just about us overcoming psychological problems. Once you start to feel less anxious and stressed, and are living out your new core beliefs, it may be time to look again at your life.

Take the opportunity to look at how you live your life, and see whether you can do so more positively.

Feeling fine about human fallibility

Perfect people don't exist. You're human and hence fallible – you make mistakes. Deal with it. You will make mistakes. Everyone does.

Here's some common reactions to making a mistake:

- putting yourself down
- making yourself feel ashamed and depressed about mistakes
- insisting that you must do better
- writing yourself off completely

When you do, you have a choice. Instead of your usual reaction, learn to face up to your fundamental fallibility or imperfection.

If you can, it'll be more freeing than you can imagine.

To see how much this is affecting you, answer the questions below honestly, with as much information as you can. As you do so, consider some recent events that you're putting yourself down for.

- How is putting myself down affecting my mood?
- How is putting myself down affecting my behaviour?

Exercise: My Feeling Fine about Fallibility Form

Review the event/events again.

Now ask yourself the following questions:

Did I do something bad or behave poorly?

....

Did I make a mistake or fail at something?

....

Considering my human fallibility, can I take a more compassionate or forgiving view of myself in light of these recent events?

....

....

How might I make amends for poor or bad behaviour, if appropriate?

....

....

How can I rectify a mistake or failure, if appropriate?

....

....

....

In light of these events, are there conditions I can strive to improve/change?

....

....

....

In light of these events, are there elements of them that I can strive to accept as they are?

....

....

....

How will accepting myself as fallible motivate me to get on with solving my problems ?

....

....

How will accepting myself as fallible benefit my mood and self-opinion?

....

....

Work-life balance

Balancing our work and personal life is something that most of us struggle with. It can be an ongoing project, in and of itself.

Our work-life balance has a huge impact on our emotional, mental and physical wellness.

Take some time, about 25 - 45 minutes, to complete the following questions in order to create your very own plan for a better work-life balance.

Keeping the different aspects of your life fairly balanced can help to ensure that you don't overdo some things and neglect others.

Base your answers to these questions on a weekly average over the past month.

How much time have I spent on self-help or continued CBT practice?

....

How many (if any) days have I worked later than usual or taken work home with me?

....

....

How often have I taken some form of physical exercise?

....

....

How many times have I been out socially?

....

....

How many evenings/weekends have I allocated to spending time with friends and/or family?

....

....

How many hours/days have I spent on hobbies or activities that interest me?

....

....

How do I usually relax in the evenings?

....

....

....

How much time have I allocated to taking care of household duties?

....

....

What other activities have I spent my time on?

....

....

....

....

Reflection

Reflecting on your answers to the above questions, answer the following questions:

Which activities could I benefit from devoting more time to per week?

....

....

....

....

Which activities could I benefit from spending less time on per week?

....

....

....

....

Which times/days can I allocate to neglected activities in the coming week?

....

....

....

Now look at your answers.

Where is your time is mostly allocated? Is it work? Social? Is it balanced or is there something you can do to inject more balance into your life?

Perhaps you're wondering where you'll find the time to do more exercising, studying, or socialising - or any of the activities that you're currently not doing enough of?

Just try slotting these pursuits into times when you're usually just watching television, browsing social media or working late.

Again, this is a work in progress. To continue progressing, revisit this chapter regularly to see how you're doing.

16

THE PROBLEM WITH SELF ESTEEM

Rating ourselves as 'good' or 'bad', a 'success' or a 'failure', 'worthy' or 'worthless' on the basis of our achievements or circumstances is extremely common.

Just because it's common practice, doesn't make it good practice. In fact, attaching your self-opinion to external conditions is at the very root of self-esteem problems.

Life is unpredictable and prone to change. Your mood and view of yourself can shift wildly, if you consistently anchor your value to your job, relationships, financial situation, and so on.

Your opinion of yourself is vulnerable to plummeting, if your existing state of affairs isn't maintained. That is a dangerous state of affairs.

Even the term self-esteem is problematic. It implies that a person can be given an accurate overall rating or 'estimate', even if the person doing the rating is you!

Assessing a piece of jewellery or a diamond and estimating its overall market value is easy. People, however, are living, changing creatures and far more complex than inanimate objects.

An alternative to self-esteem is the concept of *self-acceptance*.

CBT encourages you to stop giving yourself overall or global ratings altogether. Rather, accept yourself as a fundamentally worthwhile person and only rate individual aspects of yourself, your lifestyle, behaviour, and so on.

In this chapter we expand on the concept of self-acceptance and offer you some practical exercises for applying an accepting attitude toward yourself and those around you.

Learning To Accept Yourself

All human beings are equal in worth. Stop for a moment and consider how much you agree with that statement.

Isn't all human life sacred? Isn't that why murder is a crime, regardless of who's killed?

Most of us believe human beings have intrinsic value and worth. We believe we're valuable and worthy just because we exist. However, we often behave as if some people are worthier than others.

We can attach too much importance to, or overvalue, certain things prized in western society, such as wealth, physical appearance and social status.

We may mistakenly assume that people who possess these prized conditions or traits are superior to ourselves or others who lack them.

At the same time, we may attach too little importance, or undervalue, other aspects of our personhood, such as generosity, social responsibility, and kindness.

Comparing ourselves to others on the basis of external conditions, leads us to feel superior or inferior, in turns. Both positions are unhealthy because you're either putting yourself or others down.

One of the first steps toward self-acceptance is noting particular conditions to which you typically attach your self-worth.

Read through the list below. The list includes some external conditions that people frequently judge their overall worth against.

Check off the ones that resonate with you, and add any of your own that are not included in the list.

External Conditions Checklist

- Academic or educational qualifications
- Career or job success
- Creativity or artistic talents
- Ethnicity
- Fame or celebrity status
- Family background
- Intelligence
- Mental health
- Parenting skills
- Physical attractiveness or fitness
- Physical disabilities
- Physical health
- Quality of relationships
- Religious observance
- Social popularity or social ease
- Socio-economic status
- Wealth or material possessions

Now that you've pinpointed the areas that you tend to give yourself a global rating on, you can use this knowledge to help yourself overcome low self-esteem and to adopt self-acceptance instead.

Example:

You may be an excellent cook and a poor driver while your neighbour may be the exact opposite. You're still both worthy individuals, you just have different limitations and strengths.

We're all unique, we all have something to give. Instead of being critical of yourself, learn to celebrate your unique gifts and strengths.

Self-acceptance can stop you riding the roller coaster of self-esteem, which is often dependent on factors outside your control.

Learning self-acceptance, and acceptance of others, means that you're able to recognise that we're all equal in worth but unequal in specific aspects.

17

A NEW NORMAL

We've explored how to use CBT to manage and reduce your anxiety. You may be wondering what happens next.

Over the next few chapters we'll explore a relapse prevention plan.

We'll plan a new work-life balance and you'll have the opportunity to imagine a new normal. A new way of being. A new approach to life. A life without anxiety.

The next time you find yourself in a situation where you feel afraid or under threat, consider the following guidelines.

Step 1. Be Empowered!

When finding yourself in any situation, try to identify where you may have some responsibility for events that happened, or for how you respond to the event.

Taking responsibility is *not* about blaming yourself or others for a negative event or situation. You're not fault finding, as such.

Rather, taking responsibility is about empowering yourself to change a negative situation. You can do this by problem-solving, where possible, or alternatively adapting and adjusting to conditions.

Step 2. Be flexible!

Being 'stuck in your ways' can indicate rigid and unyielding ways of thinking about life.

The more rigid your personal rules about yourself, others, and the world, the more vulnerable you are to be experiencing emotional disturbance and life problems.

Rigid thinking limits your ability to creatively adapt to changing life circumstances. This attitude also leads you to avoid taking risks of any kind.

If you want to change from rigid to flexible thinking, you need to acknowledge that 'want' does not equal 'have to get'.

If you want to succeed at a task, but don't insist that you have to succeed, then you're thinking flexibly and leaving room for error. This is a healthier route, than your old rigid thinking.

Step 3. Be Realistic!

Life is a jumble of positive, negative, and neutral events. Moreover, life isn't always fair. Sometimes things happen that are undeserved.

Life just doesn't seem to stop and consider who deserves a good or bad thing to happen to them at any given time. Rather, life events seem to occur in a pretty random way.

Dwelling on unfairness can ensnare you in unhealthy emotions and prevent you from making things better for yourself.

Sometimes taking a second to consider whether what you're experiencing is truly 'unfair' or more accurately 'bad', 'unfortunate', or even 'tragic' is worthwhile.

That's not to say that unfair things don't happen, because they most certainly do. However, life is unfair to everyone from time to time, not just to you.

Step 4. Be Brave!

Sometimes mistakes are well-worth making and risks are worth taking. The trick is to be able to 'go for it' when you think doing so is in your best interests, believing you're able to cope with the consequences of any mistakes, poor outcomes or bad decisions.

If you believe that making mistakes is unacceptable, then you'll be unlikely to take any form of risk, for fear of failure.

Accepting yourself as a fallible human being, capable of both success and failure, can help you to take worthwhile risks.

Step 5. Be Self-Accepting!

If you believe that you've got to be approved of by everyone you meet, then you'll run into emotional trouble.

An approval mentality means that you'll probably spend a lot of time:

- worrying about what others think of you
- trying hard to please others
- abandoning your own needs and opinions
- becoming a bag of nerves in social setting
- losing your spontaneity, or
- acting in ways that you think will impress others.

You stand a far better of chance of enjoying social interaction, making meaningful relationships, and expressing your own unique personality, if you regard approval from others as a bonus rather than essential.

Accepting yourself doesn't mean becoming vain or arrogant and disregarding the opinions of others completely.

Self-acceptance means seeing yourself as an equal to others and being comfortable in your own skin.

18

LIVING LIFE WITHOUT LABELS

Have you ever said or thought any of the following about yourself?

- I'm inadequate
- I'm weak
- I'm a failure
- I'm unlovable
- I'm useless
- I'm bad
- I'm inferior
- I'm worthless
- I'm no good
- I don't matter
- I'm stupid
- I'm pathetic
- I'm a loser
- I'm disgusting
- I'm crazy

The names you call yourself can erode your sense of worth and reinforce negative core beliefs. Another term for name calling is *labelling*.

Leaving behind loathsome labelling

In addition to unhelpfully giving yourself negative ratings, you probably call yourself names, and nasty ones at that. You may call yourself names silently in your own head or you may sometimes say them out loud.

Even if you don't think that you always really mean the hateful things you call yourself, they can have a negative impact on your self-opinion.

If you don't mean it, don't call yourself it! And even if you do mean it, stop it! It's having a bigger impact on your mental health than you imagine.

The main method of losing loathsome labels from your life is to resist using them. It's like breaking a bad habit.

Catch yourself in the act and refuse to call yourself those labels, whether that's inside your head or out loud.

Instead of calling yourself globally negative labels like those just listed, try to label only your actions instead.

Be very specific about what aspect of your actions you're displeased with.

Example:

Instead of saying 'I'm a total loser,' specify what you've lost by saying something like 'I lost my job', 'I lost the golf match' or 'I lost the promotion'.

Being specific helps you to accept that you're capable of losing sometimes, but acknowledges that you're also capable of winning sometimes.

Hence no one is ever a 'total loser'. Certainly not you.

Loathsome Label

Here's some loathsome labels you might have used about yourself in the past:

- I'm inadequate
- I'm worthless
- I'm weak
- I'm no good
- I'm a failure
- I don't matter
- I'm defective
- I'm stupid
- I'm unlovable
- I'm pathetic
- I'm useless
- I'm a loser
- I'm bad
- I'm disgusting
- I'm inferior
- I'm crazy

Here's some healthy labels you can replace those loathsome labels with:

- I have skills and talents
- I'm a worthwhile person
- I have both strengths and weaknesses
- I have many good qualities
- I'm a fallible human being capable of both success and failure
- I have significance
- I may have certain defects, like any person, but I'm not defective

- I can do stupid things sometimes but that doesn't mean I'm stupid
- People can love me, and I am worthy of being loved
- I have capabilities
- I do many useful things
- I'm a normal person who can both win and lose
- I'm a person with both good and bad traits
- I'm acceptable
- I have equal worth to others
- Even if I sometimes do crazy things, I'm not totally crazy

Take a moment to list some healthy alternative statements that you will generate to replace your loathsome labels:

....

....

....

....

....

....

....

....

....

....

To reinforce your belief in them, write them out. Practice saying your healthy alternative statements out loud to yourself several times every day.

Make a point of doing this in situations in which you would typically resort to loathsome self-labelling.

Example:

You notice that people treat you differently. You start thinking, "I'm crazy".

As you catch yourself thinking this, replace this your healthy alternative, saying "I'm a creative thinker, unique and gifted. Unlike anyone else." Say it out loud, if necessary.

It can help to drown out your old ways of thinking, replacing them with a healthy alternative.

Choose to act as if you truly believe your healthy alternative.

For example, if you truly believe 'I'm worthwhile', then you'll start to act differently.

This might include doing things like looking after your health, joining in social activities, voicing your views and opinion, and making eye contact with others.

The more you act according to the new way you want to think of yourself, the more you will come to believe in its truth.

In order to successfully change a habit. Research suggests that you need to stick with it for a minimum of three weeks.

After one week, you'll start to notice changes. You'll need to keep on practising alternative healthy ways of thinking about yourself for several weeks to create a habit that sticks.

With deliberate effort and practice, thinking in positive and balanced ways about yourself will become more automatic.

In other words, you'll have developed a new constructive thinking habit.

19

PREVENTING RELAPSE INTO
OLD WAYS

There are two common reason for problems reappearing.

First, is a lack of awareness and second, unrealistic expectations.

When we think about relapse, we often imagine spiralling downwards rapidly into old ways and habits, sometimes becoming worse off than before.

However, relapse can start in a very small way. Relapse can start with one small step back towards an old behaviour, or a step towards a replacement behaviour that is just as destructive.

Dealing with anxiety is not a one-time thing. In order to manage and prevent relapse you must be diligent.

Even though you've put your very best efforts into reading this book and completing the exercises within it, you'll still need to remain mindful of the challenges, the triggers and the subconscious need to protect yourself.

At the end of this chapter, there is a worksheet with guidelines that you can use to develop your own personalised relapse prevention plan.

Do you want to give yourself the best possible chance of a positive outcome? Not just for now, but for the foreseeable future?

Yes? Then take the time to plan your new way of being moving forward, whilst being realistic about the possibility of relapse.

Just like anything else in life, if you don't use it, you will lose it. If you don't practice it, you won't remain good at it.

Let's take a look at the road to recovery and how it impacts your future mental and emotional health, and how as a part of this journey you can prevent relapse.

Relapse is different for every person. For some it looks like total surrender to anxiety and sometimes being in a more challenging state than before. For others it looks like hidden behaviours and rituals, with the justification of having it all under control.

In reality, when trying to reduce anxiety and improve your mental health, you can expect to have difficult periods or to experience setbacks .

The road to recovery is not linear. It doesn't happen in a straight line, but in more of a zig zag pattern.

Sometimes you may move forward and make great gains. At other times you may have to move sideways to maintain your gains. At other times you may take a step back in order to take a couple of steps forward in the future.

When this happens, remember that this is a normal part of recovery. And however it happens, relapse is to a certain extent also a part of recovery.

Some see a relapse as a test of your new skills and learnings and others see relapse as an absolute disaster.

By preparing for setbacks, by being realistic about relapse, you can in fact manage the thinking patterns and behaviour that arise as a result.

Be compassionate with yourself when experiencing relapse, rather than giving yourself a hard time about it.

A relapse is not the end of the world, it's just a bump in the journey.

Use the tools that you've already learned, go back through the exercises and apply what you've learned.

The Road to Recovery

Develop a daily practice of mindfulness.

Whether through formal or informal sessions, continue to journal and give yourself the time and space to process emotions and feelings.

It is important that you see your recovery as a new baby, one that requires nurturing and protection. You may decide to create a schedule of regular brief sessions for yourself, rather than one long session every morning or evening.

Don't take your improved mental health for granted. Keep practising your new ways of thinking and related behaviours. This will help you maintain your health and well-being, reducing the chances of, or completely preventing, a relapse.

For example, if you make changes to your thinking, but then return to old unhealthy ways of behaving, you put your gains at risk.

Consistently acting in line with your new beliefs can help you to stay on track.

<u>Exercise - Trouble Shooting</u>

Panicking or catastrophizing about relapse, or even about any obstacles, new challenges or occasional setbacks, can lead to severe bouts of anxiety, which in and of itself can make you feel hopeless.

Use the idea of a setback as an opportunity, to further consolidate your understanding of core CBT techniques.

This, the first step in your relapse prevention plan is about, troubleshooting. The idea behind this exercise is to help you spot potential setbacks before they truly take hold.

This will take no more than 10 - 15 minutes of your time. It will help you to develop a strategy for those unwanted thoughts or emotions that come up when you feel panicked or challenged.

Step 1

Close your eyes and recall the ways of thinking, feeling, and acting that have previously maintained or worsened your target problems.

Step 2

Now try to imagine scenarios that may come up in the future that may trigger these old unhealthy ways of thinking, behaving, and feeling.

Step 3

Next imagine yourself coping successfully with your trigger situation by thinking and acting in constructive healthy ways.

Exercise - Something old, something new

Because CBT focuses on goals regarding your problems, it also recognises the benefit of working toward broader goals, based on what's important to you.

One of the major keys to keeping yourself on track, and preventing a relapse, is to have a very clear understanding of what is *actually* important to you.

Your life values, not those of others, are what will help you in the darkest moments and give you the hope you need to pull through.

Acting in line with your personal values, and engaging in activities that you enjoy or consider worthwhile, helps you to stay psychologically healthy.

Now that you're on the road to recovery, take some time to build a value list here.

Your list is something that you can review daily, weekly and maybe eventually monthly. This may grow as time goes on, but do the best you can right now to understand what is important to you.

This written exercise can be completed and can take between 30 - 45 minutes, or longer if you have the time.

Example:

Sofia believes that we are all responsible for the planet and that everyone can do their part by recycling, lowering their carbon footprint and learning about climate change.

She may not be a full member of the Green party, but she believes that there is a problem, and that we must work together as a collective to solve it.

This would put environmental Initiatives high on Sofia's list of values.

Consider the following regarding your social views:

- Social and economic equality

- racial and cultural equality,

- environmental initiatives

- new style of education

- freedom of speech in the truest sense

Add your own here, no need to stick to the list, make them your own:

....

....

....

....

....

....

....

Example:

Rebecca is big on manners and while she doesn't want to engage in demand thinking, she believes that if you treat others the way you want to be treated then the world would be a kinder place.

This would put 'kindness and generosity' and 'treat others as you want to be treated high' on Rebecca's personal values list.

Consider your personal life values here:

Here's a list of some life values.

- Treat others as you want to be treated
- Kindness and generosity
- Being thankful and appreciative
- Facing issues head on
- Averse to confrontation
- Live and let live

Feel free to write your own, these are just to inspire you:

....

....

....

....

....

....

Example:

Jonny strives to be very empathetic in all of his relationships. While he is a great listener and is often referred to as understanding by family, friends and colleagues alike, he sometimes wishes that others heard just as much as he heard them.

This would make 'To be empathetic not sympathetic' and 'to be heard and hear others' high on Jonny's relationship values.

Consider your relationship values:

- To be heard and to hear others
- To operate out of love and not fear
- To be empathetic, not sympathetic
- To be supportive, when possible

Write your own here, these are very personal and so will really need for you to dig deep:

....

....

....

....

....

Consider your family values:

- Put family first
- Be loyal to family
- To respect family

Take some time with this one, and remember family isn't always about DNA. Sometimes 'family' includes the family you choose for yourself.

....

....

....

....

....

....

Consider your broader values:

What values do you hold for my community, the human race, and the planet?

- World peace
- Health and well-being for all

Feel free to add your own, these are just to get you thinking:

....

....

....

Once you've completed your list of life values, you can then move forward to decide on the specific action you can take to express these values in your life.

For each value, answer the Where? When? With whom? How often?

When you take the time to consider what matters to you outside of yourself this can lead to you developing a purpose.

Realising that you have a passion, can help you to engage in meaningful activities. This, in turn, keeps you motivated and gives you a reason to further your recovery.

If your hobbies and interests have been neglected due to your psychological problems, now is the time to reintroduce them.

Restart practices that you used to enjoy and that gave you a sense of achievement.

This can be anything from joining a community group, to recreational study, spiritual practice, reading, writing, creativity, outdoors, sports, whatever appeals to you.

Exercise - Your Anxiety Prevention Plan

Your recovery from a life of anxiety requires a plan. Your plan includes how to deal with relapses, setbacks and unexpected challenges when they arise.

Your well-being is paramount.

As you complete the plan below, take the time to really think through your answers.

Each section requires 15 - 30 minutes to complete, so you may want to complete this in stages and really take your time to make this plan as robust as you can.

This plan can be revisited regularly, perhaps monthly. As you revisit it, you may find that things have changed for you and others, or you may have developed further insights.

Section 1: My Personal Commitment

What is my primary problem?

....

....

....

What are my goals for my primary problem?

....

....

....

What techniques have helped me thus far?

....

....

....

What is my helpful attitude or belief about my primary problem?

....

....

....

In what ways do I need to push myself in order to advance my progress?

....

....

....

....

Why is it worth pushing toward overcoming my problem? (Be specific)

....

....

....

How can I be compassionate with myself about setbacks and my reluctance to carry on?

....

....

....

What behaviours do I most need to resist, in order to overcome my problem?

....

....

....

What behaviours do I most need to foster, in order to overcome my problem?

....

....

....

When can I allocate time to practise CBT, both behavioural and thinking based?

....

....

....

Section 2: My Support Network

Who in my life is most likely to understand my current problems?

....

....

....

What specific forms of support do I most need right now?

....

....

....

Which specific friends or family members can I seek support from? (List their names here:)

....

....

....

....

What kind of support am I most likely to get from each of the people listed?

....

....

....

Who can I approach for professional help?

....

....

....

What support groups can I join or look into?

....

....

....

Section 3: My Reality Check

Identified negative event or situation:

Which people or conditions contributed to the negative event or situation occurring?

....

....

....

....

....

Can I take a degree of legitimate responsibility for what occurred?

....

....

....

How can I take personal responsibility for my emotional and behavioural responses to the negative event or situation?

....

....

....

How might taking appropriate personal responsibility, help me to resolve the event or situation or adjust healthily to it?

....

....

....

Section 4: My Surrender Report

Detail a negative situation or event (past, present, or future):

What aspects of the situation am I trying to control?

....

....

....

What aspects of the situation am I trying to gain certainty about?

....

....

....

....

....

Are these aspects of the situation within my range of control?

....

....

....

Is it possible to be certain about these aspects of the situation?

....

....

....

How are my attempts to gain control and certainty affecting my ability to adjust to the situation or event?

....

....

....

....

....

Aspects of the situation or event that I think are unfair

Am I mislabelling any aspects of the situation as 'unfair' when to view them as 'bad', 'unfortunate', or 'tragic' is more accurate?

....

....

....

What arguments can I use to convince myself that accepting life's potential to be unfair is in my best interest?

....

....

....

Section 5: My Risk Assessment

Risk I'd like to take but am avoiding:

Why am I avoiding taking action?

....

....

Realistically, what's the worst thing that could happen if I take this risk?

....

....

....

Can I imagine surviving the worst possible case scenario?

....

....

Is it worth it to me to take this risk even if I don't get my desired outcome?

....

....

....

If so, why?

....

....

....

Make a diary note to revisit this plan in 4 weeks' time.

You can evaluate how things have changed, and see if you have any further insights.

20

GOAL SETTING

CBT uses the power of goal setting to help people decide and then maintain a healthy recovery.

After all, if you don't have realistic goals based on what is important in your life how can you expect to achieve your goals?

In order to set effective goals, begin by answering the following questions:

What is my problem situation?

....

....

....

....

What is my healthy negative emotional goal?

....

....

....

....

What sorts of actions are typical of this healthy negative emotion?

....

....

....

....

What specific actions can I adopt that fit with my emotional goal?

....

....

....

....

How will carrying out these actions be helpful to me?

....

....

....

....

You may return and add goals as you understand more about your own personal triggers.

Structuring your goals

Your goal statement should include:

- Your problem situation or trigger
- Your emotional goal
- Your behavioural goal

Example

Here's the format of your goal statement:

My goal is to feel [emotional goal] ... about [situation or trigger] ... and to act [behavioural goal]

Now complete it for yourself:

My goal is to feel (emotional goal):

....

....

....

about (situation or trigger):

....

....

....

and to act (behavioural goal:

....

....

....

Now you're ready to make a concise problem and goal statement. Making goals very specific will increase your chances of achieving them.

It's important to include the following in each of your goals.

- Where?
- When?
- With whom?
- How do I want to feel?
- How do I want to behave?

Follow the guidelines below, as you begin to set your goals for overcoming anxiety.

- Positive: How can I state my goal in a positive form?
- What do I want to work toward feeling?
- What do I want to work toward doing?

Observable: What changes will I notice when I am getting closer to my goal?

- how will I feel differently?
- what will I be doing differently?
- what changes might other people in my life notice?

Realistic: Is my goal concrete and within my reach?

- how hard will I need to work to achieve my goal?
- do I have the necessary skills and resources to reach my goal?
- can I visualise or imagine myself reaching my goal?

Timed: What is a reasonable timeframe to set for achieving my goal?

- when can I get started
- with goal-directed behaviour?
- what days and times can I devote to carrying out goal-related tasks?
- when and how often will I review my progress?

When you are ready to set your goals for your new life, share them with close friends and family to help hold you accountable.

TAKING THE THEORY AND CREATING A NEW REALITY

In this book, we've tried to provide you with the core skills and techniques to help you overcome your emotional and psychological challenges.

If you've taken the time to read through this book and follow the exercises, then you should start to reap the benefits.

If you've read through it but not completed the exercises, stop and go back through, completing them as you go. This will ensure you get the full benefit of using the CBT approach.

Going Forward

Anxiety can be disruptive. It can be all-consuming, and present as an almost relentless series of challenges.

As you go forward, there will be times when all your best efforts don't seem to be enough. This doesn't mean you haven't made progress or that CBT for anxiety doesn't work.

It simply means that you are human. You're just as vulnerable to setbacks and obstacles on the path of life as anyone else is.

It's time for you to you move forward with your life, creating a new normal.

You are well-armed. You have the knowledge and information you need to take on your greatest psychological opponents, win each battle and eventually the war.

Two Self-Defeating Strategies

Requesting reassurance and seeking safety

There are two common self-defeating strategies for dealing with problems, that people suffering from anxiety often employ:

- looking for ways to secure your safety
- asking others to reassure you that the worst won't happen.

Why don't these strategies work?

The reality is that your problem is insecurity – not a real danger or threat. The more you look for reassurance and seek safety, the more anxious and unsafe you'll feel in the long term.

Example:

For example, if your partner reassures you that he or she isn't about to leave you, you'll feel better but only for a very short time because you can't be reassured.

If you're told that the plane won't crash, or your job is safe, you'll believe it for about ten minutes before you start obsessing and worrying again. Nothing sinks in for terribly long.

You can't be convinced that you're safe. The answer to this conundrum is to accept the possibility that your partner could one day leave you (even if that situation isn't terribly likely). Or accept that your safety will be compromised, and that you'll survive or not.

Stop seeking safety and reassurance from others. No-one can give you guarantees.

Listing the people that you most often approach for reassurance, can help you recognise your self-defeating habits.

As a rule, we tend to wrestle reassurance from the people we're most comfortable with, such as partners, close friends, and family.

Resisting this urge can help us to learn to give ourselves reasonable reassurance and may improve our relationships with those close to us.

Try re-focusing your attention onto how the people you care about most are feeling. Ask them what's going on in their lives rather than using them solely to quell your fears and anxieties.

Here's some questions to ask yourself:

Who do I go to for bouts of reassurance? List the names of specific people:

....

....

....

Does this reassurance last for more than a few hours or days?

(Answer Yes or No only)

....

How do I try to safeguard my safety? List specific actions:

....

....

....

....

Who do I ask to try and guarantee my safety?

List names of specific people:

....

....

....

....

Do I then feel safe for more than a few minutes or hours?

(Answer Yes or No only)

....

Do I end up going through the same safety and reassurance processes over and over again?

(Answer Yes or No only)

....

What does this tell me about my attempts to make myself feel safe and reassured in the long term?

....

....

....

....

....

....

Is it a long-term solution?

(Answer Yes or No only)

....

How might resisting the urge to seek safety and ask for reassurance benefit me in the long term?

....

....

....

....

Can I learn to accept uncertainty?

....

....

....

....

Stop Self-Medicating

When Feeling Better Stops You from Getting Better

Often attempts to make yourself feel better, only bring about the kind of results you most want to avoid.

We think that a little drink will take the sting out of your guilt, anxiety, or depression.

We believe that a little extra dose of a sleeping tablet might quiet your anxious mind, stop the flashbacks, or quell intrusive images. Can't argue with that.

We all like to take the edge off our uncomfortable feelings, which is understandable, but not always helpful in the long run.

For example, if you desperately try not to be socially awkward, you may well end up being so self-conscious that you say something odd or behave in an aloof manner.

That scenario is just one example of how trying to feel better in the 'here and now,' can actually make you worse in the 'there and later'.

Cease self-medicating your mood

Drugs and alcohol are pretty effective mood-altering substances – in the short term. But be warned, these immediate interventions have long-term ramifications.

You could end up addicted to sleeping medication or dependent on alcohol. Or you may just feel more depressed and anxious the next day when you wake up with a hangover. That's not fun.

Self-medicating habits can extend to normally innocuous activities such as shopping and watching television.

Anything you do to distract yourself or deal indirectly with a core problem is termed *self-medicating* in psychotherapy.

Self-medicating behaviours can include anything that you do for immediate relief or gratification. Usually anything that you're doing too much of, can be classed as such a behaviour.

Exercise:

Take a look at this checklist below.

Be honest with yourself and consider which of these self-medicating behaviours you currently engage in:

- shopping
- drinking
- dating
- sleeping
- watching TV
- sex
- reading

These behaviours can become problematic solutions if done too much or in lieu of other more productive behaviours.

So, check out your motivation for whatever you're doing – as honestly as possible.

Answer the questions below to determine which behaviours you can commit to change. You can use some of the options listed or come up with your own.

How do I self-medicate my mood?

....

....

How does this affect my mood in the short term?

....

....

How does this affect my mood in the long term?

....

....

....

What other effects does self-medicating have on my life?

....

....

....

A Setback is simply a pause

If you're recovering from anxiety, whether that's panic attacks, a compulsive disorder or anticipatory anxiety, it's likely you'll experience a setback.

When we take the time to re-program the mind and our emotions, it is an ongoing process. As such we will all experience the occasional slip back into old ways of thinking or being.

As life continues to unfold, we'll be faced with new events, challenges and even traumas, that may trigger old patterns of thinking and behaviours.

Remember, change is not linear. It happens in more of a zig-zag pattern than a straight line.

Life is all about ebbs and flows, some days will be so good you'll wonder why you ever struggled in the first place. Other days will be so challenging, you may feel as if all of your efforts have been for nought.

This is OK. In fact, it's what you should expect and be prepared for.

Imagine a day when you will feel the urge or notice yourself getting lost in your head again.

Plan for this happening, and decide right now, what your best course of action will be in this event.

Will you practice a mindful meditation? Will you repeat one of the exercises here in this book? Perhaps you'll call one of your support networks and talk it through with them.

Forewarned is forearmed.

You probably won't catch yourself every time you have a setback or face a new challenge. Being prepared and familiar with the tools can give you the confidence that whatever happens you will somehow be OK, and you will figure it out.

Planning how you will manage when you face a setback means that you can be realistic about your new life balance.

Do not over stretch yourself. Don't allow yourself to become overwhelmed by too much work. Manage others expectations, along with your own. Schedule regular check ins with your health care professional or the people in your support network.

This is your new reality, so it's up to you to make it work.

In the previous chapter we looked at relapse prevention plans. Have yours close to hand, not because you expect a relapse, but because you want to be prepared for one, if it shows up.

Think of it like having a manual for a new gadget or program. Until you know how to use it inside out and have it operating smoothly, you may want to refer to your manual every so often.

Recovery is all about repetitive practice. It requires your patience, even if you think you don't have much and overall persistence.

However long it takes is how long it takes. There is no time frame on this. There is no end game. This is about choosing to live your life a new way, with ongoing progress. Think of the zig zag, every small achievement adds up. Every hour. free from anxiety, makes a difference.

Focus on the journey and living your new reality according to what you have found works for you.

Nobody is Perfect

Whatever happens you are not alone. Nobody in this world is perfect. In fact, the word perfection should probably be erased from your personal dictionary.

We are all working on ourselves, we are all striving to live better lives and most of us are trying to be better people.

You are not alone in this fight. Millions of other human beings are struggling with the same symptoms and struggles as you, every single day.

There is no need to feel odd or strange, or as if you have an insurmountable problem. Your supporters will be there for you. You are not in this alone and no matter how bad things may get for you, there is really no need to judge yourself. No need to feel guilty.

You have the tools now to make the changes necessary. Simply take a deep breath and make the moves necessary to get yourself back on track.

You're human. As humans, we're prone to make mistakes. Rather than putting yourself down, try treating yourself with compassion and understanding.

Be kind to yourself when you're feeling fragile. Be firm with yourself when you know you are trying to opt out. Treat yourself the way you would a good friend or loved one.

So, now that you are fully prepared, expectations are set, go ahead and create your new normal. Live the new reality that works for your life, first and foremost.

Remember this, you are a valuable member of the human race. You are complex and complete, just like everyone else.

You have a purpose and a reason to live. Your life can be fun, adventurous and filled with excitement once again.

Enjoy the journey!

2 2

ONE MORE THING

If you've enjoyed this book or found it helpful, please take a moment or two to leave a rating or review.

If you'd like to start putting mindfulness and meditation into practice, you can find relaxing guided meditations to listen to on Audible.

Just search "Mindfulness Meditations - Mike Carnes". You'll discover some guided meditations that take you on a journey, to help you learn to relax and focus on the present moment.

A GUIDED MEDITATION SCRIPT FOR BEGINNERS

EMBRACE THE POWER OF MINDFULNESS FOR SLEEP, RELAXATION AND STRESS REDUCTION : RELIEF FROM ANXIETY, WORRY, TRAUMA & PANIC ATTACKS : FIND INNER PEACE AND A QUIET MIND

A GUIDED
MEDITATION
FOR BEGINNERS

EMBRACE THE POWER OF MINDFULNESS FOR SLEEP, RELAXATION AND STRESS
REDUCTION : RELIEF FROM ANXIETY, WORRY, TRAUMA & PANIC ATTACKS
FIND INNER PEACE AND A QUIET MIND

PAUL ROGERS

1

GUIDED MEDITATION AND AFFIRMATIONS FOR ANXIETY

You're going to take a journey, becoming relaxed and aware of your surroundings.

Before we get started, make sure that you are sitting or lying down in a comfortable position.

You don't have to lie down or sit cross-legged. Simply find a place where you feel comfortable and sit in a way that makes your body feel relaxed.

Whatever's happening, you have the power to control your breathing.

First, exhale completely through your mouth. You should make a whooshing sound.

Now, breathe in through your nose while counting to four, 1, 2, 3, 4.

Next, hold your breath while counting up to seven, 1, 2, 3, 4, 5, 6, 7.

Exhale slowly through your mouth, while making a whooshing sound again, this time making sure to count for longer, up to eight, if you can.

Let's do that again, focus on the sensations of breathing, as you do so.

Breathe in deeply.

Now exhale, making a whooshing sound.

Breathe in through your nose. Hold your breath for a moment.

Now, exhale slowly, making a whoosh sound.

Breathe in, slowly and deeply. Hold your breath for a moment.

Now exhale, with a whoosh.

Breathe in through your nose and .... exhale with a whooshing sound.

Breathe in again and hold, 1, 2, 3, 4, 5

Now breathe out and release any tension in your feet and toes.

Breathe in again.

Hold for ... 1, 2, 3, 4, 5

Exhale and release any tension in your knees and thighs.

Breathe in slowly and deeply and hold 1, 2, 3, 4, 5

Breathe out, releasing any tension in your chest and glutes.

Breathe in deeply and hold, 1, 2, 3, 4, 5.

As you exhale, release any tension in your arms and hands.

Breathe in and hold, 1, 2, 3, 4, 5

As you breathe out, release any tension in your neck and jaw.

Inhale and hold, 1, 2, 3, 4, 5

Now breathe out and release any tension in your face and eyes.

Gently close your eyes.

Focus on nothing but your breathing. Feel each breath you take entering your body, filling yourself with as much air as possible.

Let the air sit in your body for a moment, as if it were full of flavor and you were sucking the juices.

As slowly as you can, let the air leave your body, feeling the small stream against your throat and mouth. As the air leaves your body, feel it against your skin, whether the stream hits your upper lip or your chest.

Feel your body relax. Your shoulders are weightless. Though you are holding yourself up, you can still feel as your body floats through space and time. You are not held down by anything.

You are light. You are free.

Remember this feeling of weightlessness as you continue to be aware of your breathing.

Let your shoulders drop until it feels like they can't relax any further.

Breathe in and out, making sure that your shoulders remain weightless. Let your stomach relax as well.

Focus on your breathing, feeling the breath flow in and out of your body.

2

IT'S TIME TO GO ON A JOURNEY

You're going on a journey in your imagination, to somewhere relaxing, peaceful and safe.

Before you lies a bright, sunny beach. You can feel the warmth of the sun shining on your face, its warmth starting on your face and spreading to the rest of your body.

You look down at your feet to see that they're partially buried in the sand. You wiggle your toes around, feeling the small grains of sand.

As you breathe in, you become aware of the scent of the sea and the sounds of the waves. The water is crashing against the shore, and as you breathe out, you hear the leaves rustle with the wind.

The beach is empty, except for a small child sitting close to the shore. The sun is bright, and the air is refreshing.

The beach is quiet, and no one else is in sight of this child but you. The child does not look in your direction and sits alone, staring at the empty water in front of you both.

There's nothing here but you, the child, the wind, the water, and the beach.

As you approach the child, you notice that they're holding their knees to their chest and burying their face, so that you cannot see their face.

You can sense that they aren't afraid of anything here on the beach, there is no danger or threat here. And yet you sense some form of fear in them.

You reach out your hand, feeling theirs gently falling into yours. You can feel the way their hand begins to warm yours once you begin to touch.

The child turns it's face to you, no longer as fearful, as they were just moments ago.

You both look at the water for a moment, the blue sky spreading over your heads. There's not a cloud in sight.

The child still seems uneasy, so you lift them up into your arms, holding them tight.

They're trembling slightly. As you hold them closer, you start to breathe slowly, in and out. You breathe in, then out, holding them close to your chest, so close that they can feel your breathing.

You feel yourself relaxing and the child senses this. The child starts to breathe in time with you, breathing in and out, in time with your own breathing.

(sound of breathing in and out)

The breathing calms you both, and you begin to relax. Both you and the child stare out at the water, the sounds of the waves lapping on the shore and the warmth of the sun on your bodies helping to relax you further.

Here, you feel fearless and full of joy. The child smiles at you.

Yet you can see by the look on the child's face, there is something still on their mind. They lift their hand, pointing in a different direction.

The child wants to show you something. You can see something in the distance, but you're not quite sure what.

You set the child down, hoping that they will lead you to the place they want to show you.

As you look towards the end of the beach, you see a small shack come into focus.

The child steps out towards the shack, walking in front of you. In their excitement, they begin to run.

The child can sense that you're close behind them. With each step you take, you feel the sand beneath your feet. As you lift your foot, you feel the hot sand once you place it down. The sand and sun warms you with each and every step.

Your feet eventually bring you to the shack that you saw from a distance. As you stand right outside, you can see how much larger it is than what you thought in the distance.

The shack has clearly been here on the edge of the beach for a while. Pampas grass has grown around the sides, and a small gravel path connects the entrance to the edge of the sand. There are marks and scratches on the side of the building, each telling a different story.

The child takes you by the hand and leads you inside. There are no lights, no furniture, and no windows.

The child begins walking around the shack slowly, while you stand by the door. Instead of wondering why the shack is here or who it belongs to, you look around you to discover more.

Along the walls are buckets, tins, and containers filled with shells. Each bucket is different, and every shell is unique. You walk over to one of the buckets, picking up a handful of shells in your hand.

Some of the shells are small and conical. Others are large and flat. Each shell once had a purpose. It belonged to something. Once it might have been a safe space for a creature, now it's a decoration on the beach.

The child tries to pick up a particularly attractive bucket of shells, but they struggle to lift it. You don't know why the child wants to pick up one of the buckets, but you walk over and help without question.

You lift up the bucket, and the child leaves the shack. The door remains open, and you step through. The child runs towards the edge of the beach, dipping their toes into the shallow water.

You walk a little slower towards them, feeling the sand beneath your feet once again. You can't tell how many shells are in the bucket. Maybe hundreds, maybe thousands.

Just as there is an endless amount of grains of sand on the beach, there are a seemingly endless number of shells in the buckets of the shack.

All of these shells were once important, they served a purpose, but they are no longer needed.

Once they were growing living things, able to carry life. Now, they are nothing but physical memories of what they once were.

Yet, they still hold beauty. Though they have sharp edges and smell of the sea, each one is beautiful, in it's own way.

Each shell has it's own crevices, cracks, and holes. Some shine under the sunlight, whilst others sit lacklustre. Each shell has it's own unique design.

You look down at the shells and see more than just old houses for snails and crabs.

You start to realize that each one of these shells represents one of your fears, worries or anxieties. All of the moments of worry, stress, anger, resentment, and jealousy have manifested themselves into these shells.

You look at the child and realise that they know exactly why the shells are here and what each shell represents.

The child picks up one of the shells and throws it into the waves. They smile and beckon to you. Somehow you understand what they're doing.

The shells don't want to sit in buckets in the shack anymore. They serve no purpose there anymore. They should be released back into the depths of the ocean.

They must be thrown back into the ocean, where they can crumble and break into sand. Sand that might get pushed onto the shore. Sand that will be under someone else's feet one day. They may still hold some beauty, but that fades. That doesn't have a purpose anymore. They will become sand one day, and you understand that it's better to do so in the open water, than in the empty dark shack.

One by one, you and the child throw the shells away. Each time you lift a shell, you feel the weight in your hand. You feel the crevices and cracks that differentiate each shell. You throw one into the water, hearing the plunk of the waves as the shell sinks to the bottom.

Once one bucket is empty, you go back to the shed to get another. You and the child both take turns throwing shells in until there are none left.

By throwing the shells away, you are casting aside your anxieties. The fear, hate, negativity, and stress are all now in the water, getting washed clean by the strong, blue waves.

No longer will the shells sit in a bucket anymore. No longer will the old worry and stress that you've been carrying take up space in your mind.

As you walk back to the shed, the child is standing there alone. You reach out your hand again, and they place theirs into yours.

You don't offer your hand out of fear now. Instead, it's to lead them out of the shed.

Neither of you has to be in there anymore. It serves no purpose and holds no meaning. The shells are gone, so now it is time for you to go as well.

You look again at the child and realize that something about them is very familiar. They have bright eyes, an innocent smile, and their face is full of curiosity and wonder. You can see that they are impressionable and that they have so much life left to live. They have so much to learn, and you want to protect them from all the fear and hate that they might experience.

You lead the child to the edge of the beach and they open their hand, revealing there is one shell left. You take it from their palm, looking towards the water. As you look at the child again, you realize that it is you. It is your inner child.

It is a familiar shell, one that will remind you of this moment. One that you feel has meaning. One that is comfortable. You know that you cannot hold onto it. It will serve no purpose. It must go into the water with all the others. You walk towards the water and throw the last shell in, throwing it as far into the water as you can.

As you turn around, the shack has gone and so has the child.

You are alone on the beach.

You can feel the sun warming your face. The wind is still blowing the leaves, and the waves are still crashing.

You continue slowly breathing in and out.

You are peaceful. Your mind is clear, and there is nothing left to do.

All is well, and you feel safe and calm.

You feel clarity, calmness and peace.

You have the power to embrace these feelings whenever you choose to. To return to this beach, at any time.

You are at peace, and your life, in this moment, is calm.

You are at peace with yourself. You are at peace with the world. You are at peace with those around you.

You are at peace with your inner child.

LETTING GO : A PATHWAY TO INNER PEACE, SERENITY AND SURRENDER

A GUIDED MEDITATION FOR RELEASE OF ANGER, HURT AND THE PAST

LETTING GO

A Pathway to Inner Peace, Serenity and Surrender
A Guided Meditation for
Release of Anger, Hurt and the Past

PAUL ROGERS

LETTING GO

Welcome!

It's time for meditation, and that means you're invited to unwind, kick off your shoes, and to feel completely free and easy.

Before we start, let's make sure everything is prepared. If there happens to be a lot of tension and nervous energy in your body right now, then it might help to shake out your limbs, and take a few deep breaths.

Shake your arms out vigorously, and do the same with your legs. Get rid of some of those kinks and muscle knots along your spine. Roll your shoulders, and try to relax those muscles around your neck, and feel your whole body come alive.

If you want to, you can tense up your whole body, right down into those core muscles.

Hold it there, as tight as you can... and then let it all go... like a big sigh of relief.

Tense up, nice and tight, then *let go* completely... Feel those cares begin to melt away... Make sure everything is loose and easy.

* {...allow some time...} *

If at any time you start feeling light-headed, then just take it easy, and breathe normally until you feel steady and strong again. Go at your own pace, you don't have to prove anything, or accomplish anything at all...

Before you settle down, remember to clear your lungs, your throat and your sinuses, so your breathing feels completely light and open.

Now, get as comfortable as possible.

Lie down on your back, and place your hands on your tummy, one hand over the other, an inch or so below your navel, more or less.

* {...allow some time...} *

Let's begin by coming fully into the present moment.

Turn that powerful beam of attention inwards, and begin to settle your mind. Become fully aware of what's going on right here and now. Take in your surroundings, and try to beam out a relaxed and friendly sort of feeling towards everything around you.

Examine your state of mind... What kinds of thoughts are coming up? ... there's no need to pay those thoughts any attention – no need to jump onboard the train of thought, or analyze anything – just notice your thoughts, acknowledge them, greet them, and come right back into the present moment...

Notice what kinds of emotional feelings are present in you right now ... accept them... No need to fight them... we're going to let go completely, and trust the natural process...

Sense your whole body from head to toe... Acknowledge what it feels like to be alive, and present.

Breathe – you're allowed to just *be* – exactly as you are... Simply be present. That's enough.

Enfold yourself in a sense of acceptance and compassion. Allow yourself enough room to exist, just as you are...

Notice the glow of life inside you, however faint it feels. Without forcing anything, encourage those feelings of well-being to envelope you.

Allow everything to happen as it will, naturally. Let go of the need to control it. Whatever happens is perfectly acceptable.

Let the tip of your tongue press lightly against the roof of your mouth, relax your tongue, your jaw and face, and breathe comfortably and naturally, in and out through your nose. Relax your eyes, relax your brain, and relax your entire body.

Each time you exhale, *let go of your breath completely* ... sinking deeper and deeper into it. Just allow it to happen, and make sure you're not holding on unnecessarily.

Feel the breath coming in and going out. Pay close attention, without tensing anything. Feel free.

Forget about yesterday, and forget about tomorrow, just for now.

As you begin to relax more and more, allow your mind to become still and alert.

Rest your weary mind and heart. Let go. It's All Right.

Bring your attention to where your hands are resting on your tummy. Let your tummy rise and fall with your breathing. Sense your spine near that spot, from the inside, and locate your center. Imagine that you are pulling the breath towards your center as you inhale ... and let go totally as you exhale.

Become aware of your heartbeat.

Take your time, there's no rush.

As you're listening for the sound of your heart, your mind is becoming quiet.

Take a long, delicious moment to scan your entire body from the tips of your toes to the crown of your head. Sense your skin, and feel the atmosphere all around you. Smell the air, and feel it washing in and out of you, as you breathe comfortably, effortlessly.

Allow your heart and mind to become open, and emotionally receptive.

2

IT'S TIME TO TAKE A JOURNEY

Close your eyes.

Feel yourself sinking deeper and deeper into relaxation, as if you're becoming weightless. Allow your limbs to become completely motionless and still, as if your body is going to sleep, but your mind remains completely alert, and at peace.

Imagine that you're dissolving completely... It's a wonderful feeling.

As you're breathing, the air is washing away all those knots and all those feelings of heaviness and weariness. You're sinking into the earth beneath you, becoming nothing but a single point of consciousness, completely free and alive. Allow it to happen, it's all right, simply let go...

Let go of your resistance, and allow your imagination free play for a while. Just go with it for the moment. Let go of the past, and forget about the future, and become one with the journey. Your body is safe and comfortable, and there is nothing in the world to worry about, just for this moment...

Let go of the limitations of your life for now.

You're expanding beyond your individuality and your personal world, and you're becoming a part of something big; something awesome, inspiring and miraculous.

As you're breathing in and out, imagine the whole universe breathing with you, in perfect equipoise, in perfect rhythm. Feel your consciousness expand, embracing all life, all time, all of space, everywhere and everything, all at once...

Your consciousness is expanding beyond your body, filling up the whole room. You're a part of the air, and the earth, the walls, and the roof, and they are a part of you. Let go of the stuffy confinement of your ego. You're becoming nothing but a wisp of air...

Now you are expanding beyond that, and up into the sky above you, and all around.

You're light as a feather, free and relaxed, and you can go wherever you want to go. There is a friendly and inviting atmosphere everywhere, as if every atom in the cosmos is alive and awake, curious about your journey, and everything wants to help you...

Open your heart and your mind to all possibilities. Feel yourself drifting up into the air, high above the earth which spreads out like a tablecloth beneath you. See the rooves of the houses, and streets below... the tops of the trees, the hedges and the landscape disappearing off towards the horizons, all the way around you. You are a part of the sky, limitless and free.

Your mind and heart are opening wide, accepting the whole world, and feeling the connection to all existence. The whole neighborhood acknowledges you, accepts you, and wishes you well.

Somewhere down below, on top of a wall, you can see the tiny form of a cat, and it seems to be aware of and watching you.

As you drift along above the rooftops you're filled with a sense of joy. The world looks very different from up here.

Everything is glowing with an ethereal kind of light, and everything seems to be pulsing and alive. Down below you can see the tops of the trees swaying gently to and fro, and you can see people going about their lives.

As you're drifting peacefully above it all, you notice that you seem to be connected to things by means of thin, insubstantial strings, or lines. They are almost like fine threads of light. They are holding you up, and protecting you. You can use them to move around, and to explore wherever you want to.

One of those strings of light goes down towards the cat. It's still watching you, almost as if it's inviting you to pull on the string, and see what happens.

So that's exactly what you do. The moment you tug on the string, you find yourself being pulled gently towards the cat, and moments later you're right there beside it. It looks at you with unblinking eyes, watching to see what you will do. It's almost as if it wants to communicate with you.

Somehow you know exactly what the cat means to say, even though neither of you needs to say a single word. The cat knows that you're on a journey, and it knows you've come to learn the art of letting go.

This is going to be your first lesson.

With exquisite feline grace, the cat begins to move from where it has been sitting. First it stretches out its entire body, the way cats do when they have been sitting for a long time.

It seems as if the cat wants you to pay attention to that stretch. It's about to jump up onto the top of the roof of the house, and you can see the path it is intending to take. You can see exactly where it will walk, how it will jump, and where it will land.

Taking one last look at you, the cat turns, and with a series of quick, fluid moves, it leaps up a wall onto a tiny shelf, and leaps again onto the roof.

In one sudden burst of energy the whole movement is accomplished, and the cat turns to look at you again, as if inviting you to follow. It walks along the peak of the roof to where a chimney sticks out, and then leaps up on top of it. There it selects the perfect spot, and stretches out lazily on top of the bricks, gazing out across the yard below.

You drift up to where the cat is lying, and as you do so, you send out a friendly greeting, without words, using only your feelings. As you approach, the cat begins to purr.

Not a trace of tension, not a single bit of wasted energy, the cat is completely relaxed, at ease, and alert.

"This is how you let go", it seems to be saying, with eyes half closed. Somehow you know exactly what that cat means. Words are completely unnecessary.

All around you the strings of light are curling away, off into infinity. You are aware that you can travel anywhere you want to travel using those strings of light. The cat seems to have lost all interest in your conversation, so it's time to move on...

One particular string of light catches your attention. It is thicker than the others, and seems to be swirling in the most mesmerizing way. The light seems to be calling to you, so you tug the string, and in an instant you're off, drifting high above the world again.

This time you drift towards a wooded area, thick with trees and greenery. The string of light pulls you along, and you land in the center of a grassy knoll, in between the trees.

Here there is an old tree stump, and as you drift down towards it, you can see that it must have once been a mighty tree. The string of light seems to be coming from the stump, and before you know it, you've landed right next to it.

You're in twilight time, free from the boring limits of the regular world, so as you focus your attention on the tree stump, you can go backwards and forwards through time at will. You can see how the tree once sprouted from the ground, and you can follow its whole life from seed to sapling, as it once grew tall, and stretched up into the sky.

You can see the many seasons that have all passed, as the tree grew thick and strong. You can feel the life of the tree connected to you, and you can feel its roots deep below the ground, and the tips of the leaves at the very top of the tree, each and every one. You can sense the passing of many years, even though you're not moving at all.

You can see how the tree grew very old, and finally one day it was cut down. You can feel it falling down to the ground with a crash, and you can feel each part of it, branches, bark, stem and leaf.

You can see the woodcutters sawing the wood. You can see where each plank that was cut ended up – some became part of houses nearby, and others were made into furniture. Smaller branches were cut up and used for firewood, and the ones that stayed behind became homes for termites and grubs.

Five generations of caterpillars became butterflies there. An old man carved a wooden toy out of another knotty piece, and gave it to a grandchild, who cherished the toy for years.

You can feel the life of the tree in each and every part – and there is no sense of anger or regret about any of it.

The tree accepts all, lives through all, and forgives all. This is another lesson for you – forgive, and let go. This too will pass.

Your heart begins to open as you contemplate the life of the magnificent tree.

For years it stood, accepting all, one with all. Years passed like moments, and moments were as years. Many seasons ago some seeds fell nearby, and these have already grown to full size, and you can feel their life, as if it was your own life.

You feel the green sap, the roots seeking out water, and all the twisting branches, as if they were a part of you, like your own hair and fingernails

Now it feels as if you are a leaf on the tip of one of the branches, budding from a green shoot, slowly becoming yellow, and then gradually becoming brown and dry.

The trees seem to be whispering joyfully together: Let go, let go.

So you let go, and the leaf is caught up by the wind, and now you're floating up above the world again. It feels as if you have lived a hundred years as a tree, even though only a few moments have passed.

Your world is expanding, and you are part of something vast and mysterious. Open your heart, and take it all in.

Feel your consciousness expand, until you include the whole planet earth in a friendly, welcoming embrace. Expand as far as you can, and include as much of the universe in your mind and in your heart as you would like to.

Let go of your own limited worldview, and in your imagination, become one with everything that exists. Here there is no need for fear or regret, worry or bitterness. Here you can be free.

Now your journey takes you high over a great mountain range.

You can see the snowy peaks far below you, glistening in the soft light. Following another string of light you drift downwards, and alight on top of one of the highest peaks.

You sense the immovable strength beneath you, and millions of years of rock under your feet. There is something uplifting and majestic about these mountains.

It feels as if they are the bones of the earth, and a part of your whole being. You can sense the lifetime of the mountain range, spanning ages, as they pushed up from the earth, year after slow year.

Here on the high peak everything is covered in snow, and you can see for many, many miles in every direction. Millions of subtle shades of colors dapple the landscape, reflecting and changing as you watch. You feel peaceful and warm, even though the air is so thin and cold. You're miles from nowhere, with not a soul in sight.

Flakes of snow are floating in the air, tossed this way and that way by a playful gust of wind. The snowflakes seem to be calling to you: Come and play!

Before you know it you're tumbling with the snow, and next thing you're sliding down the mountainside! The voice of the ice and snow seems to be saying to you: Let go! Let go! Fall down with us!

So down you tumble, with a great rumbling and crashing, sliding down into the valleys below, without a care in the world. This is how you slide, this is how you let go, this is how you flow with life...

Now you're melting like ice, and trickling down the mountainside between rocks and through gullies and canyons, becoming a swift-flowing stream.

Now, you're dropping down a waterfall into the deep pool below, and racing onwards, as the little stream joins up with a larger stream, and still larger one, flowing strong and clear through the mountains.

On and on you flow, gurgling and splashing your way down towards the levels plains far below. Nothing can hold you back, nothing can keep you prisoner.

Now you are the wide, slow-paced river, flowing sedately through fertile lands...

Now you are a fisherman in a boat on the stream, and now you are a child jumping from a rock into the refreshing, cool water. You are the shrieks of joy as you splash into the water.

Time is flowing, flowing like this river, and you are everywhere, and everything all at once. Now you are a washer-woman rinsing a bright yellow dress by the banks of the stream, singing an ancient song in a language you don't understand. Now you are a silver fish making its way upstream. Now you are a dragonfly hovering over a still pool in the sunlight...

You are the river, forever moving, never stopping.

You are letting go, again and again, of everything you ever where and everything you will ever become. The past cannot hold you, for you are a child of the timeless present moment.

It feels as if you have lived countless lives, each one like a distant dream, each one with its own story, its own sorrows, and its own joys. You're letting go of all of them, with love, gratitude, and appreciation.

You allow them to float and bob away from you, floating down the river. Soon, they become dots you can barely see in the distance.

Now you are the mother saying goodbye to her adult child, who is leaving for distant shores. You are letting go, with love.

Now you are the small child in the back of the car, luggage in tow behind, leaving the town you grew up in, heading to an unknown future. You're letting go again, and flowing with the river.

You are a young man returning to his country of birth, after years of wandering the earth, making one mistake after another. You're leaving that life behind, and letting go.

You are a refugee, a dancer, a wild child, a cancer survivor, living your life to the fullest possible extent, letting go of the pain you've endured.

You are the farmer whose crops are destroyed in a flood, starting over, letting go of the past.

You are the battle-weary soldier saying goodbye to his lost comrades, learning to let go of the hate and fear.

You are the grandparent, saying farewell to your family. You are the college graduate, saying farewell to the past, and embracing an unknown future.

You are a billion people living different lives, letting go of each one, accepting, loving, forgiving, and flowing on and on forever...

You are all of this, and yet you are none of it. All that exists is this single present moment...

Finally you begin to feel that it is time to return to your own life...

With an open heart and a grateful spirit you tug on the string that connects you back home, and in a moment you're back where it all started.

As you slowly return to your body, think about the amazing journey you've just experienced, and try to see your own life from a new perspective now.

Remember that you are free, in your essence. No circumstance can ever change that. As you return to your normal routines, remember that the past is the past, it can no longer hold you prisoner. Let it go.

Remember that your cares and worries come from the things you love and want, and that these too will pass. Let them go.

Whatever hurtful emotions remain with you, whatever negative habits come back to you, keep letting them all go, again and again and again. Keep embracing the present moment, with the best attitude you can muster.

Letting go doesn't diminish you in any way. You do not become less of a human being, in any way when you let go of those troubles. They do not define you. They cannot own you. You're allowed to just let them go.

Whatever your past, whatever has happened to you, and whatever choices you have made – those things don't define you in any way. Your mind and your heart are infinite.

Forgive yourself on the deepest level for whatever you feel you may have done wrong.

Release any anger, deep sadness or pain. Let them all go.

Accept yourself on the deepest level, because you are more mysterious than even you can ever know.

Love yourself deeply, from the heart, for you are an amazing, miraculous part of the grand cosmos.

Open your heart.

Be present, here and now.

Feel the life inside of your body. Feel it radiate out to your extremities, elbows, hands and feet, and beyond. Feel the warmth, and try to sense the pulse of your heart.

Sense the entire length of your spine now, from the root, right up to the place where it joins the skull.

Notice where it feels tense, or where it feels painful. Hold your attention on those areas, one at a time, and as you're breathing, feel the tension begin to melt away, and the pain begin to dissolve as you let go, and let go, again and again...

Open your eyes, and come back to full, alert consciousness.

And don't forget to stretch like a cat when you're ready to get up!

GUIDED MEDITATION FOR ANXIETY SCRIPT

THE POWER OF MINDFULNESS, AFFIRMATIONS AND BREATHING TECHNIQUES FOR STRESS RELIEF AND TO HELP OVERCOME ANXIETY

WELCOME TO THIS MEDITATION

Let's start by turning off any mobile devices, making sure you're warm enough and won't be distracted.

You may want to lie down, or sit with a straight back on a chair or meditation cushion.

(Pause)

Bringing your attention to your nose now . . . beginning to be aware of your breath.

Feeling the air flowing in and out . . . and your body relaxing a little more - on each outward breath.

(Pause)

Your mind and body are connected.

Focusing on an anxious thought is like a trigger - it signals your nervous system to react to a threat . . . causing your body to go into fight - flight - or freeze mode.

Your can reduce anxiety and heal yourself so that you can relax and sleep peacefully.

By noticing anxious thoughts as they come up ... and changing them to thoughts that support your well-being.

(Pause)

Noticing how you're feeling now.

Accepting yourself - just as you are.

Knowing that any feeling is fine.

Just noticing.

(Pause)

There's nothing to do right now.

This is your time - breathing and allowing yourself to be.

Safe ... sheltered ... supported ... accepted.

Letting go of the outside world. It's not important - here ... now.

Any sounds around you - will gradually begin to fade . . . as you breathe.

Feeling your breath flowing into your chest and belly . . . and out again.

Noticing the rise and fall of your belly.

Attention tuned in ... to the rhythm of your breath - like gentle ocean waves ... rolling in ... and out.

Time doesn't exist here.

(Longer Pause)

Guiding your mind now, to notice your body - part by part.

And relaxing each part on the way.

(Pause)

Starting by tensing the muscles in each part mentioned, then letting them go, noticing how they feel when they relax.

Now - tensing all the muscles in your right arm while making a tight fist with your right hand.

Keeping your fist clenched as you breathe in ...

And as you breathe out - releasing the hold and allowing your hand and arm to give way to gravity.

Noticing how your hand and arm feel as they relax and the tension within them dissolves.**(Pause)**

Tensing all the muscles in your left arm while making a tight fist with your left hand.

Keeping your fist clenched as you breathe in ...

And as you breathe out - releasing the hold and allowing your hand and arm to give way to gravity.

Noticing how your hand and arm feel as they relax and the tension within them dissolves.**(Pause)**

Tensing all the muscles in your right leg and foot now as you breathe in ...

And as you breathe out, releasing the hold on those muscles.

Noticing how your right leg and foot feel as they relax and the tension dissolves.

(Pause)

Tensing all the muscles in your left leg and foot now as you breathe in ...

And as you breathe out, releasing the hold.

Noticing how your left leg and foot feel as they relax and the tension dissolves.

(Pause)

Now clenching all the muscles in your stomach and buttocks as you breathe in ...

Breathing out and releasing your hold.

Noticing all the sensations as these muscles relax.

(Pause)

Bringing your attention to your shoulders.

Raising them up towards your ears as you breathe in ...

Releasing the hold as you breathe out, feeling them drop and give way to gravity.

Tightness and tension dissolving into sensations of fluid warmth.

(Pause)

As you breathe in now, tighten all of the muscles in your face, all the muscles around your eyes, forehead, cheeks and jaw ...

Breathing out and allowing your face to unfold.

Noticing how your face feels as it lets go - and the tension there dissolves.

(Pause)

Knowing you can feel relaxing sensations in your body as you let go.

Breathing in and out to a rhythm.

Breathing in to the count of 3 or 4.

Breathing out to the count of 3 or 4.

If you like you can deepen the breath more.

(Longer Pause)

Bringing your attention to your forehead, a relaxed focus there - and imagine now . . .

Hills rolling like gentle waves to the horizon . . . green and lush.

(Pause)

Wild flowers scattered and stretching upwards towards a clear blue sky.

Their centres raised . . . soaking up the healing rays of the sun.

(Pause)

See yourself strolling among them, inhaling their scent.

(Pause)

Feeling a light breeze on your face.

(Pause)

Hearing the breeze whisper through the grass.

(Pause)

The sun's warmth soaking into your body and touching your heart.

(Pause)

Raising your mood upwards towards the expansive sky.

(Longer Pause)

Following the curve of a hill into a valley.

(Pause)

Walking down the slope as if you're gliding on air.

Towards a tree at its centre.

(Pause)

There's a stillness here, a calmness - a deep sense of peace.

(Pause)

See yourself now, lying down, cushioned in the grass under the protective bows this ancient tree.

(Pause)

Feeling the soft ground supporting your weight as your muscles unfold a little more. Letting go.

(Pause)

Feeling in harmony with the serenity around you.

(Longer Pause)

Aware now of the space in the centre of your chest, between your breast bone and spine.

This is your heart-centre.

(Pause)

Imagining now - breathing into and out of your heart-centre.

On each inward breath, see a golden light entering your chest from the serene space surrounding your body.

This golden light is pure love.

Feel it enter your heart, pure and warm.

(Longer Pause)

And now with each exhale, imagine the warm loving golden light begin to flow . . . from your heart-centre to the rest of your body.

Feel it warming you on its way.

Its healing qualities being absorbed into your body.

Into each cell - absorbing any old pain.

Healing you lovingly.

(Pause)

Inhaling - filling your heart-centre with warm golden love.

Exhaling - sending the golden light from your heart-centre - to embrace your body and mind.

Experiencing your whole being— held in pure love.

(Longer Pause)

Reminding yourself now ...

"I am relaxed, I am peaceful"

(Pause)

"I am whole"

(Pause)

"I am always enough"

(Pause)

This feeling you have now is your natural state.

Allow yourself to rest here for a few moments.

Noticing how right it feels.

(Longer Pause)

Looking up now to the sky - noticing how it reflects the landscape - just like a mirror.

See yourself lying there in its reflection ... your relaxed body ... your expression peaceful ... breathing calmly.

(Pause)

Noticing now that the sky can mirror your thoughts.

You're completely safe here. Just watching your thoughts in the mirror as if they belong to someone else.

You're a witness in this timeless space - observing your thoughts as they come and go - there in the distance.

(Pause)

Allowing a typical thought to appear now, reflected on the surface of the sky's mirror.

Noticing what kind of thought it is.

Whether it's about the past, present or future.

(Pause)

Noticing how this thought affects your physical body and where.

Whether it makes you feel tense.

How we think effects how we feel.

(Pause)

You can change your thoughts any time you want to.

You can choose how to feel.

Right now, you can stop thinking any thought that doesn't support your well-being.

(Pause)

See any anxious thought now, on the mirror's surface - getting smaller and smaller.

Losing colour now and fading - until it vanishes completely - absorbed by the vastness of the sky.

(Longer Pause)

And in the sky's clear mirror now, seeing a thought of your choice.

Seeing the beginnings of it emerge there.

(Pause)

Seeing yourself in the picture now - in this situation of your choosing.

In a place you want to be in.

Doing something you like - something positive and uplifting.

Choosing your thoughts.

Seeing all the details.

(Pause)

Imagining you can transport yourself now into that scene.

You're present in that scene now.

Looking out of your own eyes at everything around you.

Noticing all the information coming in through your senses.

Smelling the wonderful scents and tastes.

(Longer Pause)

Listening to the sounds. Background sounds. Nearby sounds . . . anything that's being said.

(Longer Pause)

Reaching out and touching something near you - feeling it on your skin.

(Longer Pause)

Noticing how your physical body feels right now.

(Pause)

Noticing how your heart feels.

(Pause)

Noticing how your mind feels.

(Pause)

Noticing any emotion connected to this thought of your choosing.

(Pause)

Maybe you can give a name to that emotion.

(Longer Pause)

If any negative thought comes up - inviting anxiety or worry, just dismiss it.

Reminding yourself that a thought is just a thought.

You can decide what to think.

See any intrusive, anxious thought getting smaller, fading and losing colour.

Getting smaller and smaller - as it's absorbed into the sky.

(Longer Pause)

Focusing again on the thought that supports your well-being and self-worth.

Reminding yourself by repeating the words:

"Anything is possible"

(Pause)

Lying on the grass again, feeling it supporting you - relaxed - safe and calm.

Breathing rhythmically.

(Pause)

And now, as you look up - imagine seeing yourself at a time in your future - reflected there in the sky's mirror.

(Pause)

Noticing this future version of yourself.

Inwardly and outwardly happy . . .

Naturally you . . .

Calmly confident . . .

Wise and strong . . .

Knowing whatever you focus on, affects you . . .

Aware of your thoughts . . .

Knowing you can decide to let go of the worries when you choose to . . .

Knowing you can focus on uplifting thoughts whenever you like.

So that you can relax your body and mind - and sleep deeply.

(Pause)

Looking at your reflection now.

Seeing this version of yourself - and noticing this how this version of yourself feels.

(Longer Pause)

Reminding yourself by repeating the words:

"I can let go of anxious thoughts"

(Pause)

"I can change my thoughts whenever I like"

(Pause)

"I can focus on solutions and positive thoughts"

(Pause)

Feeling all this with your whole body. Feel it in every cell.

Protected and cocooned in the strength of your inner self-worth - always enough.

(Longer Pause)

The sky is expansive - and can absorb any anxious thoughts.

Always there for you to breathe your worries up to . . . where you can watch them fade, get smaller and disappear.

You can always change your thoughts by noticing the beauty around you - and by focusing on what you want.

Remembering that your inner self is strong, wise and whole - always enough.

You can be aware of your body, and let go of tension.

Your relaxed body and relaxed mind, allowing you to sleep well and deeply.

(Longer Pause)

Feeling connected to your heart-centre . . . breathing in and out of this space.

The golden light entering this space as you breathe in . . .

As you breathe out - sending the warm golden light around your body . . .

Feeling bathed in love and support.

Feeling centred and full of gratitude.

(Longer Pause)

You have so much love and gratitude inside to share.

(Pause)

Imagining one good thing in your life now.

It doesn't have to be a big thing.

It could be a flower you saw - or a delicious meal you ate.

Remembering this scene in all its detail now.

The images, sounds, smells, tastes and how it felt.

(Longer Pause)

And now - with each outward breath - send gratitude out towards that memory.

See the golden light leaving your heart-centre to touch that memory with love and gratitude.

(Longer Pause)

Notice how this makes you feel.

(Pause)

Can you name the emotion you're experiencing?

(Longer Pause)

Imagining now, someone you care for standing in front of you.

And as you exhale, visualise your golden light of love and gratitude reaching out to them.

See it flowing out of your heart-centre towards them . . . encircling them and supporting them.

See this person relax and smile on receiving your love and gratitude.

(Longer Pause)

Notice how this makes you feel.

(Pause)

Can you name the emotion you're experiencing?

(Longer Pause)

Beginning your journey back now, out of the beautiful valley of your inner world.

Taking all that you've experienced with you.

To help you in your daily life.

(Pause)

Taking a long breath in ... and out.

(Pause)

Slowly becoming aware of the place you're in.

(Pause)

Sending your outward breath all the way through your body to your feet.

(Pause)

Wiggling your toes.

Sending your next outward breath down your arms to your hands.

(Pause)

Wiggling your fingers.

(Pause)

Moving your right ear towards your right shoulder, stretching ...

(Pause)

Moving your left ear towards your left shoulder, stretching ...

(Pause)

Raising your arms above your head, and feeling into the stretch ...

(Pause)

Stretching your legs out.

(Pause)

Bringing your hands towards your face and loosely cupping your eyes.

(Pause)

And at your own pace . . . whenever you're ready . . . gently opening your eyes behind your hands.